SPIDER SPECULATIONS

A PHYSICS AND BIOPHYSICS OF STORYTELLING

by JO CARSON

"Jo Carson has distilled some decades of community-conscious story collecting and playmaking into a pungent blend of narrative psychology, neuroscience, and spirit. Her work should be essential reading for socially responsible artists of every kind."

—JOSEPH SOBOL, PH.D.
Storyteller; Director of the Storytelling Graduate Program
at East Tennessee State University

"I think this profound, engaging and funny book is the very best that has been written on the topic of generating theater in communities. I use it in all my classes. My students love it."

—STEVE KENT
Director of Theatre at Univeristy of La Verne;
Founder, The Institute for Conscious Acting

"Jo Carson understands the transformative power of storytelling on both a molecular and a community level. Her genius is to be able to link the micro and the macro, and you'll be astonished at how those links get made. If this book doesn't change how you think about your own stories and the stories you want to put onstage, then, to borrow from Atticus Finch, 'You've got another think coming.'"

—LISA MOUNT
Director of Artistic Logistics; Producer and Director of
Headwaters :: Stories From A Goodly Portion Of Beautiful Northeast Georgia

In *Spider Speculations*, Jo Carson draws a web of creative connections that come to understanding after a life-altering brown recluse spider bite. By applying cutting-edge mind-body science, quantum physics and ancient shamanistic techniques, she describes how stories work in our bodies and our lives. Carson, who has an ability to capture the spoken word in her community-based work, sets down this story in her own distinctive voice, interspersing the journey with examples of her performance work.

JO CARSON lives and reads and writes in East Tennessee. A second book about her community work, a collection of favorite pieces from the story plays she has written: *Liars, Thieves and Other Sinners on the Bench*, is forthcoming from TCG in 2008. TCG has previously published another of Carson's books, *Stories I Ain't Told Nobody Yet.*

SPIDER SPECULATIONS

SPIDER SPECULATIONS

A PHYSICS AND BIOPHYSICS OF STORYTELLING

JO CARSON

THEATRE COMMUNICATIONS GROUP
NEW YORK
2008

This publication is made possible in part with public funds from the New York State Council on the Arts, a State Agency.

TCG books are exclusively distributed to the book trade by Consortium Book Sales and Distribution.

LIBRARY OF CONGRESS CATALOGING-IN-PUBLICATION DATA
Carson, Jo, 1946–
Spider speculations : a physics and biophysics of storytelling / by Jo Carson.
—1st ed.
p. cm.
Includes bibliographical references.
ISBN 978-1-55936-283-2
1. Carson, Jo, 1946–Authorship. 2. Storytelling–Philosophy. 3. Storytelling in literature. 4. Artists and community. 5. Performance art. I. Title.
PS3553.A7674Z46 2007
813'.54–dc22   2007040525

Cover, text design and composition by Lisa Govan
Cover photo by Jeremy Woodhouse
Author photo by Murray Lee

First Edition, April 2008

*Spider does not allow
discourse without storytelling:
be prepared.*

CONTENTS

SPIDER
SPECULATIONS

INTRODUCTION

(Do Read This First)

WHAT FOLLOWS in this introduction is the beginning of "The Doubter's Story" from a longer piece of work called *If God Came Down . . .* I wrote *If God Came Down . . .* as performance material for myself.

Performance material.

It is odd "performance material" because I am not usually the subject of my own performance material, and because nothing in it except the learning is the least bit dramatic. *If God Came Down . . .* is closer to a lecture told in a storytelling format. I hadn't planned to write *that*. I know how to make plays, I know what works onstage, and what I did with the material is not how you usually make plays. But some experience is compelling enough that you can't leave it alone so I wrote as I could and I played it. I still do play it.

Then, I hadn't planned to open this book with that story. But the experience it recounts (and other experiences that followed it) kept showing up as I was writing. This is the beginning of the learning that led to this book, so Mama Spider has her way, and here is the relevant part of "The Doubter's Story" from *If God*

3

Came Down . . . This is my story, the events recounted in it happened to me as reported.

> . . . The story probably begins with the big bang that began the universe, or some previous incarnation, or the day I was born, but any of those take much too long, so you just get a recent chapter. I am a playwright, my work for the past several years has centered in making plays from people's stories, so you get this as story or as play, your choice, I'm not real picky about the difference.
>
> It begins in January of 1999 in Steamboat Springs, Colorado. I was working on a series of projects that weren't working very well at all, four new plays written from stories from that community. They were my twentieth through twenty-third of the community plays I have written.
>
> In Steamboat Springs, the nice rich white folks who live there now had decided to collect heritage stories from people who can't afford to live there anymore, and those folks weren't particularly inclined to tell those stories, especially not to strangers. While we were there, it snowed another foot in the Colorado Rockies. I was the only person with the project who had driven in serious snow before, so I was driving a little rent-a-car Ford that shouldn't even have been in the Rockies long distances on roads I didn't know through new snow. It was not a four-wheel-drive car, it was not even a front-wheel-drive. There were times when I was frightened for my well-being, and I was risking my well-being for a project that wasn't working very well.
>
> I was not a happy camper.
>
> And in the town of Steamboat Springs was an American Indian art gallery, priced for the tourist trade, but beautiful things, Hopi Kachinas, silver-and-turquoise jewelry, drums and masks. I spent some time between the gallery and a bookstore next door as a respite between difficult project meetings and a boring motel room. And in the gallery was a little copper key ring

4

Kokopelli, the flute player–Trickster. I know him from the Hopi tradition, but he is not just Hopi.

Kokopelli is, among several other things, an agent of change, and I knew that.

I saw and liked the image the first time I went into the gallery but I didn't buy it because it is not my habit to presume to someone else's mythology.

Except I was really drawn to that little Kokopelli. So, about the eighth time in the gallery, and the last time before I went home, I said to myself, If you like it so much, spend the money, knothead.

When I had the thing in my hand, what came out of my mouth surprised me and surprised the clerk who sold it to me:

Kokopelli, I need some change.

"Woman, you ask a Trickster for change and you get it. May not be the change you thought you wanted, but there will be change."

That's Roe Bear. You'll hear that line again. What I meant by change was that I was not happy doing work that didn't work, that I needed some other direction or job somehow. But I wasn't specific. I just asked for change.

I flew to East Tennessee the next day, got into Tri-Cities Airport very late, came home to a chilly house, turned up the heat, listened to the phone messages, checked the mail, had a beer, and got into my bed with a brown recluse spider I didn't know was there.

Who looks between the sheets before they climb in bed? Me, now.

She bit me, low on my back about an inch to the left of my spine. I didn't know it at the time.

The progress of a brown recluse bite is not the least bit pleasant. The spider's poison kills the flesh around the bite, and people have died of these things because they can get gangrenous.

The next morning, I did know something was wrong—the bite hurt like the dickens, like a brand-new bad burn—and by the following morning, I had a hole in my back almost the size of a nickel. It would grow to old silver-dollar size before it finally began to heal. And I was lucky, the healing only took about seven months.

My ex (but not yet ex, that change is still coming) left that day for a multi-week working trip to Africa. I dropped ex at the airport and went to the doctor. My bit butt was hanging in the air for the interns to observe.

"There is only one thing that makes this kind of wound, it is a brown recluse spider bite, and this one is dangerously close to the spine."

The prescription was nitroglycerin ointment, to be applied directly to the bite.

"Good luck," said the pharmacist, "nitro is hard stuff."

Nitroglycerin, applied to the wound, would force the blood to flow in the wound, which meant, hopefully, the necrotic area wouldn't get too large, and I could keep the necrosis out of my spine. I did hope to continue to walk.

Nitroglycerin. Heart patients take nitroglycerin because it forces the heart to beat faster (thus the increased blood flow in the spider wound). It also gives you fierce headaches, and if you get too much at once, it will make you pass out. It also hurts a lot on an open wound that hurts already.

I found out the hard way that I best be lying down when I put nitroglycerin on the wound. And the prescription said twelve hours with it on, twelve hours off. I used the time off to sleep, I couldn't sleep with it on for the pain. I could pass out for a few minutes, but I couldn't sleep.

So began one version of a trip through hell.

Nothing touched the pain of the wound and the nitro made it worse, nothing touched the intense headaches made by the nitro, the passing out was frightening, and my heart beat . . . Nitroglycerin works for heart patients, but to someone who doesn't need it, the forced heart feels like a perpetual dose of fear . . .

. . . and I was alone.

Most journeys of the soul are undertaken alone.

My brother knew some Reiki practitioners, he had dated one of them. He had never been for Reiki himself but, as he said, it can't hurt and it might help.

"I'll take you."

So I went, for the first time in this journey, to perfect strangers to lay their hands on my body. This is, in the classic seeker's journey, the moment that will point the road ahead. Can't say I knew that at the time.

This was Reiki Master Sylvia Lagergren and her students' Monday night open house (give what you want in the basket at the door and wait in line). The open house is practice for Sylvia's students. There are several regulars at Monday-night Reiki. I knew nobody. I was shaking with pain. I wanted to be home, I felt like a fool.

When my turn finally came, I climbed onto the massage table fully clothed, put my face in what looked like the seat of a toilet bowl—I'd never had any experience with a massage table before—and six or seven strangers placed their hands on my body.

The first thing I felt was a surprising amount of heat coming from all their hands, some more than others. People talked over me about the events of their day until someone put a hand very close . . .

"What is this?"

There was nothing to see, I had my clothes on, he was feeling the flow of energy around the wound.

A spider bite.

"It is taking a lot of energy."

He—the voice was male—laid his hand very gently over the wound, through my clothes, his hand got really hot and the pain in the bite went away.

For the first time since the bite, about three weeks, I was pain free.

The Reiki people said turn over, and I could.

And after that, every time the Reiki people opened their doors, I was there. Do me.

I slept after the Reiki sessions like I wasn't able to sleep without it. When I'd wake up in the morning, the pain was there again, but for a few hours (great grace if you are living with pain) it was gone.

And one evening at Reiki, one of the students, a man named Joe Ortola, handed me a xeroxed invitation to a hands-on intuitive healing workshop lead by a part Cherokee man who called himself Roe Bear. I could come as a patient or as a practitioner. I put the piece of paper in my bag, more as a courtesy to Joe than anything else, I had no intention of going even though the Reiki helped. I didn't believe in this kind of thing.

Except . . .

In the time between receiving the invitation and the workshop, the ex came home, announced I was no longer significant other, or anything besides ex myself, and in fact the new significant other, a friend of mine for twenty years, had been there several times already.

Every human alive knows what betrayal is, what it feels like, and this was a double dose.

So. I went to Roe Bear's workshop because it was something to do and it was cheaper than shopping.

I went because he called himself Roe Bear, and I have a relationship with bears.

I went because I couldn't stand to be at home.

There were about a dozen people in attendance, most were energy-healing practitioners of one sort or another, most were there for Roe Bear's instruction. I was there to be practiced on. I was the second person Roe Bear invited onto the massage table that morning. I climbed on fully clothed except for my shoes. He began working on my back with a kind of acupressure, shiatsu, that finds the places where energy is blocked in the body and releases it.

It hurt more than it should have for the strength he was applying. Reiki didn't hurt. And it put me immediately on an involuntary crying jag that almost wouldn't quit. What in hell was I doing here?

Except . . .

He got to the area midway down my back . . .

"What has happened to you?" And then he said, "You don't need to tell me. Someone you love has hurt you, nothing else makes this kind of wound."

Me and my teary eyes and my snotty nose wanted to crawl under the table—there is something mortifying about failures of affairs of the heart—but it felt like being under the table might call more attention to me than had already been called, so I laid there, dripping, face down, and didn't say anything. He worked on down my back, then he got to the area of the spider bite.

"And what's this?"

Second time he's felt something on me, second time someone has felt something around the bite. Now, when I climbed on to the table, this man did not know about the ex, did not know about the spider bite. This man did not know my name, he didn't know anything about me except what he could feel in the energy around my body.

I know now, because I've seen him do it since, that in this kind of situation Roe Bear looks around the room for a person who seems needy. That morning, I was needy. He was right to pick me. I had on all my clothes except my shoes, and he had, in the course of five minutes with no conversation, by touching my back, pegged the two most pressing things in my being.

It is a brown recluse spider bite.

"That's BIG medicine."

When he finished with me, I got up from the massage table shaking and shaken. He handed me a glass of water and walked with me as I drank it.

"Are you ok?"

I don't know.

"What we've done is find places on your body where you are holding things and helping release them. You've got a lot of them right now. I expect being on the table was painful."

It had been.

I think I better go home.

"We may have changed the way you deal with anger; you won't be able to hold so much in."

That proved prophetic. I discovered quite a pitching arm in the next few weeks. And I took up a pitching practice: pitching whatever came to hand at the ex.

But that day, when I got home, I was still shaking and sick. I went to bed, went to sleep. I slept for eighteen hours, my dog had messed in the house because it was too long without going outdoors and she was embarrassed by it. If I know my dog, she had tried to wake me and couldn't do it.

I cleaned up the dog mess.

And the next thing in my mind was Roe Bear.

"A brown recluse spider bite: that's big medicine."

I went hunting for Roe Bear. I found him. You worked on me at the workshop. I left early.

"I remember. My guides said you'd be back."

In that moment, the line about the guides didn't even register.

What did you mean about the spider bite being big medicine?

In the fancy kitchen of the house where he was staying and where we were standing, a coffeemaker with a fresh pot of coffee started the gurgling that signals the end of the brewing process. He watched the coffeepot for a moment, then turned around to look at me. "What do you have to do with Hopi mythology?"

I hadn't thought about it. I hadn't remembered standing in that gallery in Steamboat Springs with Kokopelli in my hand until that moment. A gap in my world opened up.

I guess I asked Kokopelli for change.

"OH-HO! And you guess you're getting it, aren't you? Ask a Trickster for change, woman, you'll get it, you just don't get to name the change you want! My best advice is, don't say stop. Then you could really be in trouble."

It already feels like trouble.

"Call what's happened so far a little heads up."

Pay attention.

"That's it. You are not dying of this, it's just a heads up. Now, what do you have to do with language or story-telling?"

I'm a writer.

"Listen to me. Spider is a very powerful figure in Hopi tradition, she was there at the creation, and she is the keeper of language and stories, she made the alphabet in her web . . . "

A spider?

"Spider. Her name is Spider. And, right off hand, I'd say Spider has some plans for you. She bit you as close to center of the chakra for creativity as she could get without doing you permanent damage."

A chakra for creativity?

"Yes. You know what a chakra is?

No.

"Your job to find out. Now, are you dissatisfied with what you are doing these days, is that why you were asking Kokopelli for change?"

As a matter of fact.

"If I were you, I'd try to find some way to think differently about that bite, some way to think differently about the work I was doing, and I'd find some way to thank Spider."

Find some way to thank Spider. Right. Thanks for being the biggest pain in the butt I've ever had.

Except . . .

As we were having this conversation, standing in that clean modern kitchen, fresh cups of coffee in our hands, a spider–not a brown recluse–but a tiny spider on a single thread of web, dropped from the ceiling, came to eye level between our faces and hung there for a very long moment.

"Believe it," said Roe Bear.

So that's my introduction to Spider as the weaver of alphabet webs and the keeper of language and stories. Spider is bigger than just the keeper of stories (as if that wasn't big enough). In the Hopi tradition she is the female principle of creation.

The whole of *If God Came Down...* chronicles events that led, eventually, to a huge change of paradigm for me. Changing your skin is easier than changing your paradigm, it just takes some time but it happens without your thinking about it. Changing your house, your car, your clothes, your diet, your mate takes some thought, but even those are easier. Changing your mind is very hard, and I had to land in the hospital at risk of losing some body parts before I began to pay real attention to what I was learning. But I did finally pay some attention and body parts intact, I have come to think differently about energy, this world and the journey of it, and the work I do.

This book is part of what has come of the new thinking about my work and the stories of our lives.

This work, too, is written oddly. There is almost as much content in the asterisked sections as in the work itself. I'm not using asterisks quite like they are usually used. You can get the ideas presented without reading the asterisked notes, but the experience will be considerably enriched if you do read them.

In the Further Practice sections, you will find recommended reading (with notes) about the material in that chapter. You will find the proper bibliography at the end of the book.

For the second time since Spider made herself so very known to me, I'm using my own stories more than is comfortable in my writing. You can speak or write analyses to convey an idea, you can use visual illustration, or you can write or tell a story to present that same idea. Most of us have an inherent preference for one or another of these things. We learn more readily one way or another. Our brains are set up differently; there are literally different kinds of intelligence. There are certainly more than three kinds of intelligence, but when the medium is paper and print, the choices for the presentation of ideas are limited. I'm using analysis (truly speculative) in this work, but I'm depending on story. Most of us depend on story. Sometimes the best story I've got is my own, so I'm using it. Enjoy.

My Observation Position

I AM, AND HAVE BEEN for almost thirty years, a professional writer. I've been a writer longer than that, but I've made my living from the writing for almost thirty years. I am a playwright primarily, but I have been known to do whatever I can make pay. I've published books for adults, books for children, and plays. I have won a series of national awards (five different ones) for my plays. I have an agent who handles my traditional plays, and if I were trying to provide for myself from the books and the award-winning plays, I'd be homeless and hungry.

So for the past fifteen or so of those thirty years, I've been working in a niche, like an ecological niche, a place an organism can live in, but cannot live out of without some serious adaptation.

I have come to honor this niche, and it is from the niche that this book issues.

I have been working with a series of communities to develop performance pieces (plays) based on oral histories gathered from those communities. I may be the most produced playwright in this country (thirty-plus new plays onstage in fifteen years), except I am produced in places most people have never heard of, often using people who've never been onstage before.

This is not the way to get to Broadway. But then, Broadway is not where I've been trying to go.

At the beginning of one of these projects, I often help the people who are going to collect stories in a community learn how to interview other people.* I always do this story-collecting teaching if I have the opportunity because good oral histories make my job doable and there are more and less useful ways to go about collecting stories. On the other hand, sometimes I learn from a genuinely committed individual how to really go about collecting stories in a place. The oral histories are transcribed, I work at home from the transcriptions and, using every trick I can think of to make narrative interesting onstage, I put together a play.

These plays are sometimes written around a theme. An easy theme is the work of a place; loss of innocence is a harder one, but, to my mind, more interesting. Sometimes a play will have a significant community member's story as a backbone. The stories are pieced together from whatever is available in the collected oral histories. My job is to make something of what comes to me in the oral histories, to find a theme in what is there, to make it coherent in some way, to make it simple and powerful in performance, and to take an audience on a journey with the piece as a whole.

I do run into difficulties sometimes when someone already has a collection of oral histories, and I'm hungry enough to accept the project before I've read the transcripts. Mistake. These are not useful questions: "What is your favorite Bible verse?" and "What is your favorite hymn?" and "Would you sing some of it?" Questions like that do not give me much to work with. What happens in a situation like this is that I end up combing the oral histories for things like language eccentricities, searching for possibilities to write from. Most often, communities don't even realize I've made something up, but it can get difficult when people want to know where I got this or that story and the honest answer is that I made it up.

"Well, it can't be in the play because it isn't in the oral histories."

So I have a response to that problem. It started as a dismissal, but the more I've used it, the bigger the answer has gotten in my understanding: given the breadth and depth of human experience, this or something very similar happened to somebody here sometime and we need the story to make the play work, and so let's use it.

I have become, over the course of reading all these oral histories and creating all these plays, an apprentice of Spider's (if not a full assistant) in the keeping and using of stories, and I am continually astounded by human experience. Astounded.

Assuming I have good oral histories for a project, my job is to be as true to the individual story and the community as I possibly can, to stay within the realm of the acceptable in what are mostly very conservative communities, and at the same time to push the bounds of the acceptable to invite consideration of what may be difficult (murder, abuse), sometimes in very hard ways. I am almost always an outsider in these situations, I can see patterns in events and stories in a way that an insider probably never can. Also, I never know whose toes have to be avoided and that helps the writing a lot. In the finished pieces, I do not name the people the stories come from unless the community wants to do that, so specific toes are, at least, relatively anonymous.

The plays I write are then produced by the communities, often using professionals in key jobs (directors, designers) and using nonprofessional community people as actors. This poses another specific set of problems in the writing: how do I create work that people who are not trained actors can bring to life onstage? That discussion is an essay unto itself but to be brief, I play with ways narrative can be made dramatic because amateurs can handle narrative much better than they can handle scene work.

These pieces have tremendous relevance in the places where they are performed, and more often than not they have equal meaning for the people who do them. This is not traditional theater. "Not business as usual in the black box," says one of my directors, Jerry Stropnicky. It is an older form of theater, closer to storytelling when storytelling meant the stories of our lives and not Jack Tales (or the like) performed by storytelling professionals in school libraries. These events can be truly magical and it

17

doesn't matter how less than perfect the acting is. The work holds meaning in a real community-specific context and the performers have genuine investment in the endeavor: heart.

Some of these projects (like the Swamp Gravy project in Colquitt, Georgia, where I wrote their first six years of plays) have been ongoing, successful economic-development projects in places that have gotten desperate enough to think art might help economics. Sometimes it does, but not in the way people usually think it will. This art never makes much money. What it does do is change people's perceptions of their place and their community so that it somehow becomes a place worth keeping, and that can turn economics and a number of other things. Other projects are restoration-of-soul projects (my naming), like a community of Mennonites who lost farms to strip malls and subdivisions and wanted some way to help keep community and think about who they are without their traditional way of life.

As I write this book, I am working on my thirty-first and thirty-second of these community plays: a first-time play for Sautee-Nacoochee, Georgia, potentially another economic-development project; and a second play for Harlan County, Kentucky. Harlan County is ravaged by coal mining, oxycontin and other drug problems, and some desperate economics. It is, first, a restoration-of-soul project. If we can carry it beyond that, we will.**

I don't advertise anywhere as a playwright for hire. I get these projects by word of mouth; someone has seen a performance somewhere, wants something similar to happen in their community, and gets in touch with me. Sometimes I work just as a hired playwright (I'm more at risk working by myself and it is harder, but I usually learn more), and sometimes I am part of a larger production team (more fun), but either way, some individual has still had to have seen a show somewhere, and been moved enough to figure out how to get in touch with me or the team and initiate a conversation.

I have watched communities change radically for doing these endeavors, turn around economically or come again to community, at least briefly, from disinterested or disenfranchised parts. I have seen blacks and whites work together in ways that have never previously happened in a given community. And I have watched individuals' lives change radically. It is because, in a community, the process of the story collecting and the use of those stories literally grow some new roots. Then, for an individual, the process of making art—being part of producing a script which includes everybody who wants to be in it—is an approach to the realm of creative play and that can be mind-altering, life-changing stuff. Watching someone else's artistic product—a production of a play, a movie, a canvas—can be a moving experience, no question, but it is not the same as being part of the process of making art. Obviously, these plays are not the only way to engage individuals in creative process, but they are a wonderful way because risk is so shared among the participants. This creative-play business is incredibly important. Things happen in the process of creative play, left/right brain connections that weren't there before, improved learning capacity in children and adults, renewals of agency, and that is just the beginning of the list. These things are, at the very least, grist for new thinking about what art is and how we can use it in our lives, and they ought to be reason enough to restructure our educational system, but that is not the story of this book either.

There are things to think about regarding the physics and biophysics of the story business.

The beginning of this physics and biophysics thinking came with the spider bite and what felt at the time like a series of huge discontinuities. To be brief about the recovery, I am now a Reiki practitioner with some years of study in energy healing,*** Buddhism, Chaos Theory, Quantum Physics (the stuff published for the mathematically challenged), shamanism and related fields. Seven years is not long, but it has been an intense course. Except for work (I'm self-employed, so this has become a portion of my work) and time with my animals, I read and study for my own pleasure, and in the years since the spider bite, my study has been related to exploring this new paradigm and understanding and improving my own energy-healing skills. It is the most compelling study I've ever done and the most paradoxical. Much of the energy learning comes in experience. It has to be felt, and feeling isn't accomplished with just the left brain. Some of the learning is not even about understanding something, it is about experiencing it. Understanding may or may not come later, but the search for understanding can sometimes be a true hazard to the experience. Where is a left-brain reader/writer then? Lost, at least at first, I was very lost. Buddhist tradition calls the good use of this lost situation "beginner's mind." It is a useful idea, but it is hard in practice because it is extraordinarily difficult to give up enough of what you think you are or know in order to be a true beginner.

I do not miss what I left behind, and I have come to see the story work I've done for a living as a kind of healing work. I think of it that way because of the changes I see in individuals and communities who do it.

I make no pretense of truly understanding the science, I read and digest as best I can and apply the ideas to the energy kept in the stories of our lives. Nor can I make any claim to truly understanding the energy work, but I've seen things happen that might actually be called miraculous if miracles had credence in this culture. I might do better seeking my enlightenment in a cave somewhere, but I'm awfully accustomed to hot water and a microwave oven and I'm still devoted to the endeavor of trying to put words on paper in some order.

To speak about this stuff at all, I have to come up with the courage to look foolish to some, because I'm likely to do that very thing. But it is important to try to speak about what I'm seeing, so here goes.

◄ THE ASTERISKS ►

*Story collecting: I teach a process (my instruction handbook is available). The first question I ask anywhere is: "What stories do we have to tell for a play to be about this place?" That question usually includes what issues we have to address. In Harlan, Kentucky, that list included coal stories, floods, oxycontin and Trickster inclinations, i.e., how people make the best of long-term hard times. In Etowah, Tennessee, it was railroad stories and politics.

Then we (this "we" is usually a project committee of some kind and I) list people from the community known to have experiences around the specific subjects, and ask them to talk in story circles. People who had been displaced in one flood or another are invited for coffee and story swapping. It is a situation in which people with related experience speak about that experience on tape. The value of a story circle is that one person's experience reminds others of their experience and the gleanings are usually pretty rich.

I ask for story circles around all the issues named as important in any given place.

After the story circles, individuals are identified: "We should talk to my neighbor/uncle/grandmother/the railroad buff who has all those toy trains." Sometimes they are the people who were good raconteurs in the story circles. Interviewers set out for one-on-one endeavors. Interviewers take a tape deck and a release form that allows us to use the individual stories they gather. The interviewers also have some experience with open-ended questions because we've practiced using them beforehand. There is never enough experience with open-ended questions. "Where are you from?" can be answered with two words: i.e., Harlan, Kentucky, and most interviewees will answer it that way. "Tell me about where you come from . . ." asks for a lot more and is far more likely to get an involved response. "Who are your parents?" gets minimal response; "What are (or were) your parents like?" will always get more.

I try to get interviewers not to carry a set of questions to an interview. I'd rather they were comfortable enough with open-ended thinking that they don't have to have a specific list of questions. Most people want a list. So we make an open-ended question list (something of an oxymoron), a new one each time. I don't provide these questions because I want the new interviewers to think of the questions they are going to carry with them.

I teach the interview itself as a fishing expedition, a Zen exercise, go for what you get, not what you thought you were looking for. The guy with the toy trains may not know beans about the Clinchfield Railroad, but he may have an equally interesting story about how he took up with toy trains: "I had polio, and my mother bought me my first set because she thought it was something I would be able to do indoors. But it takes fine motor skills and I had to learn to use my arms and hands again to run it. I keep them now because that struggle was one of the biggest victories of my life, when I was finally able to set up that first train by myself and get it to run." If all you ask about is the Clinchfield Railroad, you are going to miss the other story entirely. So the ideal question should run: "What led you to collect toy trains?" not "I see you are a railroad buff, what can you tell me about the Clinchfield?" This is counterintuitive to the way we usually think, and it is a tremendously useful technique to learn.

The next thing I teach is how to live with silence without getting the fidgets and leaping ahead to the next question on the list. It is active listening: how to encourage a storyteller without interrupting her/his thought. One memory usually does call up another and the trick is to wait for it graciously. (A little space on the tape just makes it easier work for the transcriber.)

In selecting the interviewers, the interviewees, the stories they collect, and the performers in the eventual projects, I am looking for a level of diversity which reflects the community itself. This is tough to approach. We have divided ourselves so thoroughly by race and class and religion and age and perceived heritage that the endeavor is never perfect. But representative diversity is always a goal.

And then, I teach that you should never go to an interview looking for history. Oral histories are misnamed to begin with. When you say "oral history" people often will not talk for fear of a faulty memory because "history" has been evoked. Go on an interview to collect stories. Think and talk of the job as collecting stories. Everybody has stories.

The Newport News, Virginia, Mennonite community (I've worked with them for more than ten years) is an exception to this whole process. They are always interested in discovering ways to keep valued tradition in a changing world. They are the most adventurous of the groups I have had the pleasure to write for. The community has a literary and intellectual tradition that is very rich.

After 9-11, the Newport News Mennonite community decided it was important that what we put onstage have some relevance to current events instead of a rewrite and remount of another play we had originally planned. A committee member knew the story of a man from the community who had done "service" in the tradition of the Mennonites (nonmilitary, go where you are needed and stay for as long as you are needed) in Constantinople after WWI. There is a tradition of self-publishing among the Mennonites, so there was a variety of material available on the story. This man did his service during the time when the Ottoman Empire was being broken up, the "insult of eighty years ago" mentioned in Osama Bin Laden's video tape that was released at the time of the destruction of the World Trade Towers. The Russian Revolution was also in process when this man was in Constantinople; the supporters of the czar had fled Russia, and many were now refugees who wanted donations, but only the most fashionable donations. These were the people this Mennonite man was serving when he first arrived in Turkey. He had mixed feelings at best, his wife and children were at home making do with second-hand shoes and third-hand clothes in order for him to offer a coat in Constantinople to some Russian countess who spit on it because it wasn't good enough. But then (second act), the pacifist Mennonite farmers in Russia became targets of the Anarchists, terrorists who eventually joined the Red Army. The Mennonites' suffering was horrific. The volunteer in Constantinople was dealing with some of those people in a second wave of refugees, and he was watching the English and the French go about their systematic suppression of Islam at the same time. He wrote letters home to his wife, and she back to him. All the letters written between them were available. There were also the collections of letters that Russian Mennonites had written to family (mostly in Canada), recounting their experiences. The play I wrote, *Hand-Me-Down Shoes*, is about letting go of fear. This is an excerpt from the second act.

The Line of Refugees (three)

(New refugees come onstage. These people have walked a very long way and they were not in good shape when they started.)

JOE *(Letter writing as he watches people begin to struggle onto stage)*: Dear Alice, there are new refugees this week. We had thought of closing up shop here and going into Russia, as you know, but permission has not come to do that. There doesn't seem to be a government in Russia to grant permission. And now we are needed again here. Needed badly, these people . . .

(Joe leaves the letter and begins handing out clothes and food. There is not the order there was with the first act refugees, no cards to check. As ever, Refugee 1 is the first speaker, not necessarily the first in line.)

REFUGEE 1: Don't touch me. Do not touch me.
JOE: Don't you want to try the coat?
REFUGEE 1: Don't touch me!

(Joe hands Refugee 1 the coat and continues to work . . .)

ALICE *(Sitting at her place at the home table reading Joe's letter)*: These people are Russian Mennonites, our people, but they don't even speak Russian or English or French, just German. Mennonites have been in Russia for a hundred years and they are still speaking German? I gather that may have been part of the problem. Germany invaded Russia during the war and these people were thought to be German sympathizers. Maybe they were, I don't know. But they do not speak of the Bolsheviks harassing them, that is the revolutionary army in Russia we hear about. These people talk about a kind of mob . . .
REFUGEE 2 *(To Joe)*: They were animals, rabid.

JOE: Who were they?

REFUGEE 2: Packs of hyenas. The Anarchists. They are not with any army. You never knew when they were going to come. And there is never any reason except they have no law, and they are angry for what we had and they did not. At first, they just took what we had: grain, cows and horses. They ate the cows, and rode the horses. That way they can get from one place to another that much faster. When the grain was gone, they fed their stolen horses in our gardens till there was nothing left to eat there. They took the chickens and the pigs. We were held at sword-point while our women are forced to cook the last hen. They eat it and we are hungry. They eat our dogs when there is nothing left alive with any more meat on it. And then, there is nothing left to eat at all, and they are angry, and they murder people. Men were cut, so death was slow and painful. Women were treated worse. My wife and our child inside her were run through with a sword, but before she died, she is abused in ways I will not name and I was forced to watch. Death is better, and they know that, so they did not kill me. We might have left if she had not been pregnant, but she was. We might have left if we had not been trying to hold what was already lost . . . If we did not defend ourselves, our death was certain. If we did defend ourselves—we did not have weapons like they did—we brought their wrath upon us even harder, and we offended God as well. We have offended God.

JOE: Oh, Alice . . .

REFUGEE 2: I have lost everything I loved and walked two thousand miles. Is this penance enough? No. Most of us are already dead. I think I am one of them.

ALICE (*Reading the letter*): They are grateful for hand-me-down shoes in any size we get them, they are grate-

ful for clothes even if they are frayed and mended
twenty times, they are grateful for a bowl of beans
or a potato. They are grateful to be warm, except . . .
I think if you have been too cold too long, you can't
get warm enough. I don't know if you can ever get
warm enough again.

JOE: This is the service I came to do, Alice, it is harder
than I ever understood, but I don't care. What I am
doing has value and I am blessed to be able to be
here and do it . . . It is Friday here, and the emper-
or is allowed his once weekly trip to a mosque to
pray. The English and the French always make a
great parade out of it, so I must close this letter or
I will be held up for hours even just to get across the
road.

This Mennonite community knows about metaphor (many other
communities seem rather afraid of using it, or just don't understand how a metaphor can work onstage) and the Mennonites
want an artistic stretch in the plays I write for them. Collecting
stories with them always has to do with a theme first, and the
community is close enough to know what stories/storytellers are
likely to be important. The production committee decides who
we ought to hear stories from and makes that happen. They've
not been wrong yet.

✠ ✠

**Memory is a notoriously bad historian, and I am very aware of
that as I read and use the stories I get. I had a perfectly miserable
encounter with a county historian who told me—to make a long
story short—that artists were never interested in the facts and that
she wasn't interested in being part of something that wasn't perfectly factual. I don't know how you could ever get perfectly factual material when you are dealing with people's stories. I don't
think you can.

I do believe what is held in people's memory is often another
kind of truth, an emotional truth at the very least. And given that

I am doing an energy analysis here, the emotion a person carries from a situation or event is more important than the specific historical facts.

The stories I am using in *Spider Speculations* (besides my own) are written from stories that have been collected for the plays I have created. Some of the events can be documented with research, but I'm not writing history. When you read these stories, excerpted in this book, understand that you are reading my work created for the stage from people's stories, you are not reading the original documents.

⊰ ⊱

***One of the ways to think about how Reiki, or any of the energy-healing traditions, works is as resonance, and audible sound is an easy way to understand resonance. If I hold two tuning forks together but not touching, both in the key of G, and I strike one, making it vibrate, producing the sound waves we hear as G, the second will also vibrate and make the same sound, because it is tuned to the same frequency as the first and it resonates to that frequency.

The condition of pain or disease in the body can be thought of as a place (or system) that has fallen out of resonance with the rest of the body. When energy is applied to the body, the energy level can be manipulated until the source of pain or disease is again in resonance with the rest of the being. This is simplified, and maintaining resonance once it is restored is another endeavor. If we don't change the way we think about the things that caused the dissonance to begin with, it will return.

The other note (pun intended) is that literal sound and tones affect the energy of the body, and there are traditions (Tibetan Buddhism is one of them) that include sounds for healing. Music, and particularly singing or chanting, making the sounds aloud yourself, can change the energy of the body. So can drumming. Just as interesting is the idea that certain sounds carry or address specific energies in the body. This is not an area I have studied, except to say I've used some of what is available on CD.

Further Practice

ABOUT HEALING WITH SOUND

Ashley-Farrand, Thomas. *Healing Mantras: Using Sound Affirmations for Personal Power, Creativity, and Healing.* New York: Ballantine Wellspring, 1999.

This is a history of the mantra tradition, and the use of some specific ancient mantras. There is a CD available separately that goes with the book.

Goldman, Jonathan. *Healing Sounds: The Power of Harmonics.* Rochester, VT: Healing Arts Press, 2002.

This is Goldman's text on using sounds to heal, he's also made numerous CDs that use sound for healing. I use Goldman's music.

ABOUT PLAY

Ackerman, Diane. *Deep Play.* New York: Vintage Books, 2000.

Ackerman is always fun and surprising to read. This book is no exception. We should teach play life-long; there should be adult classes in relearning to play. I say "relearning" because most of us forget what it is to really play.

ABOUT WRITING

Hyde, Lewis. *The Gift: Imagination and the Erotic Life of Property.* New York: Vintage Books, 1983.

This is a great book but an odd one to include in "About Writing." It is somehow about *my* writing. People's stories are their property and are given like gifts, and this book started some of my thinking years ago about the work I do with communities.

FLANNERY O'CONNOR AND OLD THINKING (STILL VALID) ABOUT STORY WORK

EARLY ON, I went to the school of Southern literature: Flannery O'Connor, Eudora Welty, Carson McCullers, William Faulkner, Walker Percy, Tennessee Williams. This is not a complete list, it is a direction only. And when I say I went to school, I do not mean I sat in a classroom. I mean I read and reread what writers I loved had written.

Flannery O'Connor wrote a collection of essays called *Mystery and Manners*. When I read the book now, I skip the first and last essays: the first has to do with raising peacocks; the last, written on request, is about a saintly child who died. All the rest of the essays have to do with writing and thinking about writing and her practice of art. She is an odd teacher for me because she was a very religious woman, a Catholic in the Protestant South, and the whole of her work is informed by her Catholicism and her deep belief. I was raised (Freewill) Baptist, and escaped at the first opportunity. But Flannery O'Connor speaks to me about writing, especially in her essays. There is a short passage in "The Fiction Writer & His Country" from *Mystery and Manners* that has taught me more about good writing than any other single thing I have read on the subject. Here is the closing paragraph.

St. Cyril of Jerusalem, in instructing catechumens, wrote: "The dragon sits by the side of the road, watching those who pass. Beware lest he devour you. We go to the Father of Souls, but it is necessary to pass by the dragon." No matter what form the dragon may take, it is of this mysterious passage past him, or into his jaws, that stories of any depth will always be concerned to tell . . .

So I began to think about stories in terms of "passages past dragons," and I realized that if the story was done right, the dragon could be as little as a package of cookies in the backseat of a car, or as big as the loss of a reason to live. It doesn't matter what the dragon is, what matters is what I (as the writer of a story) understand about engineering that dragon passage. The dragon passage is the moment in which somebody (the character or the reader) learns something, acts (or chooses not to act), is not the same afterward (or contrarily, is). It is the climax in traditional terms, but the idea that it is a passage is very, very useful. Finding this metaphor, this way of thinking, was a revelation and a revolution in my writing. It has influenced all the story work I have done since, and story work includes the stories I use in the community plays.

The stories I get from communities rarely come with their passages past dragons included in them. Sometimes the passages are implied, but they are almost never included. As a culture, I have come to believe we spend time in the psychologist's office because we don't understand the idea of a passage past a dragon (or, for that matter, a passage past a puppy). We don't understand passages. Somebody else has to listen to our stories and help us find and understand those moments. A dragon passage is what gives events (and so, stories of those events) meaning, and part of my job in making plays is to supply dragon passages to the stories I use. I am astonished by this lack in people's stories, but I have known since I began this work that occasionally discovering but, more often, supplying the dragon passage is the major part of the job.

Worse: we sometimes won't (or can't) even tell our own stories. My nightmare with the community work (and it has happened often enough to be a nightmare with real meaning) is that I am handed a thousand or more pages of transcribed oral histories with no stories in them. There will be talk about events (no narrative of the event, just talk about it, and the feelings around it), analysis (list upon list of things that are wrong, and complaints about the people who make them wrong), disclaimers of the value of memory, particularly the value of the individual's memory who is being interviewed, yes and no answers to questions that want more than a yes or no answer, and no stories. Some of this has to do with the interviewer. It is why I began teaching about open-ended questions and active listening. One situation I encountered produced few stories because the project was funded to conduct interviews on a subject the local people didn't want to talk about.* Sometimes I find this absence of stories to be a geographic problem. The South, the Mountain South, and rural areas in general or, to say it another way, places where people are not so far removed from rural traditions, still tell stories. Getting stories in urban areas can be very hard. Maybe it is simply a matter of having enough time. If everybody you met wanted to tell you a story, you wouldn't get much done, so not telling stories becomes habit. But it feels like more than that. It feels like life in urban centers demands such protection of privacy that stories are somehow verboten outside intimate situations. People will sometimes just tell jokes, putting themselves in one joke after another as though what they are narrating in the joke actually happened to them, not telling their own stories at all. I've had three or four joke tellings show up as oral histories.

I've used one of these joke tellers for a play for Harlan, *Motherly Advice*. What is compelling in this man's situation is that he comes from very rural, story-rich eastern Kentucky. He left many years ago in search of a first job. He moved to Detroit (where people from Appalachia were a thoroughly despised minority by the time he got there) and he lived there most of his life. Now, tell me this joke telling is not a protective device. And truth, I prefer the joke tellers to no stories at all. I can use them.

Assuming I do have stories to work with, I give myself great permission to make art out of life. I usually use somewhere between ten and twenty stories per play. (There are exceptions to this too. My favorite way to write this work is to use an individual's story as a backbone for a play, but that never happens the first time a community does a project.) I choose from any given collection of oral histories: first, what I think I can make live onstage; second, what I can fit together thematically in some fashion while having it still be about a given community. The stories often keep their integrity as individual units: I am making a patchwork of stories. I structure each story, I work to make narrative interesting onstage, and I engineer the pieces so that they aren't just rubber stamps of one another. I provide dragon passages for all of them (they don't work as drama or story without those passages). Then, from the separate pieces, I structure the play: each story has a passage of some kind; the play itself has at least one story that is a big passage piece. The passage piece is usually a tough story: murder, abuse, a killer train wreck. It is sometimes a story that has historical importance to a place. It is always the story that has the most emotional impact in the play, and it is usually a story around which the community itself still holds old pain.

Let me give an example of a passage piece from the Mennonite community play *Cross Tides*. This was the hardest story in the play so it is the passage piece in the play. But I also made a "passage by a dragon" for the scene in the writing of it and I will point that out. This is a story of four teenage boys, friends who bought a boat together. One drove the others to pick up the boat, then drove his car home; the other three headed home on the boat. It was early spring and the water was cold. A storm came up. The boys were not experienced sailors and the boat capsized. Two of them drowned, the third boy lived. The community still mourns the loss of those young men. I wrote this story for four mothers. This is the opening dialogue.

A: My son
B: my son
C: my son
D: and my son bought a boat.

    A: My son drove his friends to get it, then he had to drive
        his car back home.
    B: My son
    C: my son
    D: and my son got on the boat.

I told the story very simply from the mothers' points of view. It
was a formal piece of theater, a ritual. Because the community is
so involved in music, I used music. My composer, Sally Rogers,
found a four-part harmony, a cappella, shape-note piece, "King
David's Lament," written from the biblical line: "Oh, Absolom,
my son, my son, I would that I had died for thee." Those are all
the words in it and they are repeated two or three times. It is beautiful, and at the same time, formal, in keeping with ritual. And it
was placed in the scene when the young men drown. It is followed by the dragon passage in the final lines of the scene.

    D: And my son . . . When my son quit fighting the water
        and the wind and the boat and the cold, when my
        son finally agreed to his own death and quit fight-
        ing, he found his feet touched the bottom and he
        found he could walk to shore.

The first year we did *Cross Tides*, the sister of one of the boys who
had drowned had to be convinced to let us use the story. Then,
she did not want her brother or the other young man named. I had
written the scene with no names, just "my son," and that is part
of what convinced her to let us use it at all. The second year we
used the story, at her request the names of the young men who
died were printed in the program. She would have liked them put
into the scene. She found the lamentation moving and appropriate. But we did not put the names in the scene because the scene,
for its content, its ritual, its lamentation, had become about every
parent who ever lost a child, and more, about the release for those
who did manage to pass the dragon in whatever way, for whatever
reasons, and come out the other side.

This is as clear an example of a dragon passage as I've got and it works on two levels: first, it was a real, physical passage for the young men (two of them into the dragon's jaws, the third past the dragon); second, it is a dragon passage in metaphor because of how it worked in the greater community and how it came to be about so much more than simply the two boys who were lost.

Structurally, in making the community plays, I go someplace dark so I can come to light again. Very simple to talk about. Harder to make work. Very, very moving in the places where the stories themselves have life.

⊰ THE ASTERISKS ⊱

*Failure notes: I've blown it three times in thirty plays. The first was with the Swamp Gravy Project in Colquitt, Georgia. I had already written six plays for them, so the truth is, I hadn't exactly blown it. They seemed (from my perspective) to think I could pull plays from a hat or some other dark place, and we were coming up on a hard deadline with a serious shortage of new stories to work from. I had begged for more stories around the theme they'd chosen, the new stories weren't forthcoming, so I got stubborn (my specialty) and wrote a pair of one-act plays called *Lost & Found* in a different format from what I'd written for them before. *Lost & Found* used a minimal number of storytellers to play multiple roles. The one-acts used two really good stories, the only good stories I had within the prescribed theme. I'd already used one of them in a different way in a previous play. I told the two stories with considerably more depth than any story I'd written previously in a show for Swamp Gravy. The play production committee decided "it's not us" without trying it onstage, and did a play I'd written previously. They did what they should have done before people got tired of collecting stories (assuming that is what happened): they fired me and found somebody local to write new shows. She didn't have to beg for stories, she already knew a bunch of them. Here's my perspective: they needed somebody new to keep faith, and at that time, local was an excellent idea. But here is the hazard: they were in the process of building a truly amazing economic development project, and when it began to be successful, they got less and less adventurous in what they would try. This is a common story, sticking to what has worked in the past without any evolution. I think not taking evolutionary risks is a huge mistake (see the section in this book on Chaos: "Three Nods to the Goddess . . .").

Lost & Found is a fine entertainment that takes an audience on an interesting journey. Great stories but . . . it wasn't them. The format was wrong. I had pushed beyond tolerance. Sometimes I think being pushy is the small print that Spider herself wrote into my job description. Sometimes it gets me in hot water. They found somebody who kept their faith, at least their format, better than I.

There is considerably more to the Swamp Gravy story now, but it happened after my tenure as playwright. The second playwright, Debra Jones, was fired after six years—is this a six-year itch?—and a playwright I mentored, Jules Corriere, is now writing for them.

The second failure was in Walton County, Florida. This was politics, and this is defiantly the PC, G-rated version of the story. One of the few things Henry Kissinger said that I really like was about academia but it applies inordinately well to community art projects, too. He said ". . . the infighting is so bad because the stakes are so small." The person in charge of oral history collection on this project was a journalist, which is different from a playwright: not lesser, just different. But it was a person who wanted to be the playwright for the project. I offered to mentor, I can help people learn how to use stories onstage, and I have had a couple of genuine successes in the mentoring business, but the offer was never accepted. The journalist was in charge of getting the stories to me, and I insisted on seeing whole oral histories instead of the journalist's rewriting of them. This turned into an on-the-phone confrontation which still didn't get me what I wanted.

I had already done one play for Walton County, *Grit and Grace*, rather successful, lots of interest and attendance. This was the second play we were working on. I got an amazing story, compiled by the journalist again (not an oral history), of a man whose boat had gone down in a storm. He had stayed with the boat and finally made the radio contact that saved the other crew members, but he died out at sea. The night of the storm—nobody on land knew yet that the boat was lost—his child at home was led upstairs and tucked into bed by him. That's what his six year old said. And she had gone upstairs to bed on her own that night without a fight which was very unusual for her. She went because she perceived him as being with her, so she didn't feel alone on her trip upstairs. A heart-wrenching story. I used that story, the boat going down, the child, I made it the central story, the backbone of the play. When I got to Florida, I learned that the story was very recent and the widow didn't want it told in the play. That's a real problem when the play is built around a story. The obvious question is why I ever saw that story at all, but that was not a question the project committee chose to ask. I had another story I could have replaced that one with, a story of a threatened kidnapping. It would have taken rewrites, but it could have been done. Instead, I was fired. The journalist rewrote my play.

The third failure is a project I quit. An assistant something (I'm not naming it) with a state humanities council (I'm not naming the state, either) decided it would be a good idea to talk about experience with the KKK in a certain small town. He wrote the proposal and got it funded without ever being entirely upfront with his local committee (a humanities project necessity) about his intended KKK research. Then, he posted contact phone numbers on flyers that he put on telephone poles throughout the county. His number was included on the list, but his number was a long-distance call, not a local one. The flyers invited people with information or stories about the KKK to call and talk. The two older women whose phone numbers were also on the posted list (local calls) got threatening phone calls. They now wanted nothing to do with the project. And they really didn't want their phone numbers posted on telephone poles around the county, and especially not in connection with the KKK.

About this time, I was approached by the same assistant to make a play of the stories he collected because I had recently done another humanities project that was a terrific success. But I wasn't told the whole story by the assistant when I accepted the project. I got to the town and found some rather frightened people and learned the real situation that way. So I said to the local committee, one at a time (they were afraid to meet together in the same place), "Why don't we just collect stories, and make a play that you can live with?" That was better as a local approach, but it wasn't what the humanities council had funded, and because of how I was connected to the project—my involvement was the assistant's idea—I was not very trustworthy in the local people's vision. I went to the town three separate times, got a few good stories, even got a couple that addressed the KKK issue. Then, I spent a very long night in a motel room with a bunch of neo-Nazi skinheads throwing assorted things—threats, beer cans and small rocks included—at my door and window. I couldn't call the police. I tried, but I had to go through the front desk to get an outside line at that motel, and the front desk person was not cooperative. "Oh, they're just having a good time." Click. This is plenty of reason to carry a cell phone, but I didn't have one then. So, it scared me. I was intimidated. Scared shitless, to be specific, which was exactly what somebody intended. Then, the theater I was supposed to be working with in the town changed the date the play was due by some months. Changed it to about three weeks from the day I got the notice. It was an impossible deadline to meet. I tried talking with the assistant humanities fellow. He'd been fired. I tried talking with the theater. They wanted to do *My Fair Lady* in the original slot because that was when they could get good singers. What? I sent the state humanities council a letter with a politer version of this story (I was trying to keep a relationship) and enough material for a one-act written and organized as a play. "You've paid me half a fee, here's half a play." I quit the project. My name is now mud with that particular humanities council. "Jo Mud." Has a certain ring to it, doesn't it?

This is a story written for that project. The material is not likely to ever be produced, and this is too good a story to leave buried in some office. The names are changed.

STORYTELLER: I was a child so it was in the forties. My sister is four years older than I am, and she says she used to hear them go by sometimes at night but I didn't, and I don't know how she would have known if it was them or somebody else. She says, "You knew, you just knew." That speaks of the kind of hold they had on people. And I heard stories, but the only story I know really happened—I mean you heard all sorts of things, but I know this one happened—this was my daddy. Our farm was divided and our house was across the road from the train station and we had a couple of pasture fields there, but the main part of the farm was about a mile on down the road next to the river. A black man bought the land adjoining that farm. Ben Jackson and his family. If my parents had to go somewhere, Ben and Lucky kept us. When we were really little, they carried us down there in old wooden dynamite boxes. I loved going down to their house, sleeping there next to the river. And Ben and my daddy helped one another like neighbors do. Well, my father woke up one morning and saw Ben and Lucky and their children standing on the platform of the train station with their belongings in boxes around them, he could see that out his bedroom window, and Daddy went over and asked Ben if he was leaving.

BEN: I am.

STORYTELLER *(As the father)*: Pardon my asking your business, Ben, but what for?

(Ben is silent.)

What for?

BEN: Some fellows been coming by. Came again last night.

STORYTELLER *(As the father)*: What did they say to you?

BEN *(Not anxious to say this)*: Said . . . said colored men didn't need to own property.

STORYTELLER *(As the father)*: Said what?

BEN: Said they didn't like me owning property. Here. Said if I wanted to live, I have to get out. My children, they're too young to do without a daddy. I love that piece of land, but I love them and Lucky more . . .

STORYTELLER *(As the father)*: Who was this?

BEN: Three of them.

STORYTELLER *(As the father)*: Who?

BEN: I can't tell you who, they had them sheets over their heads.

STORYTELLER: Daddy said he thought he knew somebody to go talk to, and he was gone the rest of the day. Now, Daddy was a man of few words. He listened close but he didn't talk much, and he was a big man and strong, so when he finally did say something, people listened. One story was about when he was foreman of a road crew and two boys came in drunk and itching to fight, and told Daddy they weren't taking any more orders from him. Daddy grabbed up a pick, threw it butt end first onto the ground, threw it so hard the pick head came off, and the handle looked like it was jumping out of the head on its way back up. Daddy grabbed the handle out of the air, turned to those boys and said, "Go home." And home they went. Well, Ben Jackson went home, too. I don't know who all Daddy talked to, and naming names now, even if I knew them, wouldn't serve anything, all involved have gone on to their reward. But one of the men he was looking for he found down at the store, so this was public. He called the man out from where he was sitting inside. Daddy said, "So and so," naming this man, "come out here." And when the man got out the door, Daddy said, "Anything happens to Ben Jackson happens to me. Do we understand one another?" And the man started in about how he didn't know what Daddy was talking about, and Daddy said, "I saw your truck tracks in Ben Jackson's yard." That was the end of it that I knew. Ben Jackson stayed on his farm. His family still has the land.

(A pause.)

Makes me proud of Daddy, so I'm glad I know the story, but Lord, it is awful what people have had to go through, isn't it?

Further Practice

ABOUT COMPLEXITY

Waldrop, M. Mitchell. *Complexity: The Emerging Science at the Edge of Order and Chaos.* New York: Touchstone, 1993.

The science called Complexity is some of the richest thinking these days about how the world works, particularly the evolution of life. This is a good intro.

ABOUT SWAMP GRAVY

Corriere, Jules and Richard Owen Geer (photographer). *A Garden of Gratitude: American Voices in Community Performance.* Philadelphia: Xlibris, 2007.

This is a picture book put together from the projects Community Performance Inc. has done.

Geer, Dr. Richard Owen. "Community Performance: Efficacious Theater and Community Animation in the Performance Cycle of Swamp Gravy Sketches," dissertation. Evanston, IL: Northwestern University, Performance Studies, 1993.

This dissertation is about the first Swamp Gravy endeavor. Geer has written further about Swamp Gravy and other community performance endeavors. He's served as director for many of them. You can find some of his writing on the internet by Googling his name or by going to the Community Performance Inc. website: comperf.com.

Jones, Dr. Debra Calhoun. "Jo Carson's Contribution to the Swamp Gravy Recipe," dissertation. Tallahassee, FL: Florida State University, College of Arts and Sciences, 2006.

Dr. Debra Jones was Swamp Gravy's second playwright, following my work with them, and she's been there for the whole process.

Swamp Gravy also has a website: swampgravy.com.

ABOUT WRITING, AGAIN

O'Connor, Flannery, selected and edited by Sally and Robert Fitzgerald. *Mystery and Manners*. New York: Farrar, Straus & Giroux, 1969.

The first essay is about the raising of peacocks, the last about a saintly child who died. You can skip those two, for my money. The rest are about her writing and she's brilliant.

The Stories

Dr. Jack Higgs told me the story about his father, their neighbor and the Klan. I have changed the names in the story for this book.

MY BROTHER
THE NEUROLINGUISTIC
PROGRAMMER, AND THE IDEA
OF REFRAMING EVENTS

My BROTHER CHANGED CAREERS a few years ago. He'd been a contractor, and at the time, I teased him about looking for indoor work. He did neurolinguistic programming training, he is now an NLP counselor. NLP is a way of working with the patterns of how we think and behave and feel, and of changing them if the change is useful. I am his only sibling and older sister, and needless to say, there were (are) many things about me that could use some changing. I came to resist anything that had the faintest hint of NLP. I even said—back during pitching practice when I was throwing things at my ex—that I had spent years cultivating some of my personal failings and I intended to hold on to a few of them. I still held to this view when he tried to tell me what I needed to do was program in some happy thoughts to get over a broken heart. We were sitting in white plastic chairs on the front stoop of my house and I was to imagine in great detail happier events, things that gave me pleasure (like great sex, he said, something that evidently gave him great pleasure, but I'd just broken up with a lover . . .). I was to put these memories on cue by imagining an event while, at the same time, pressing the tip of my index finger with my thumb, so that later all I had to do was press my index finger again to recall it. Every time hard thoughts or hurt came up, I was to press my fingers. I could do this with all my fingers, one great memory each. There is some science here in creating specific cues for memory, but I resisted this in spades.

The bottom line is that I couldn't listen to my brother on the subject of NLP. I found myself getting short-tempered when he spoke of NLP to someone else, or tried to practice what he knew in my presence. This was resistance in me, not something applied to me by him, but I had a lot of trouble listening to, much less hearing, what my brother had to say for a long time.

He'd gotten considerably more subtle in his teaching techniques, and there came a moment when I had to listen to him. He saw a performance of the play that includes the introductory spider story and he said, "Your shaman friend did an amazing job of reframing that spider bite."

I asked what he meant.

My brother said, "He didn't change what happened, but he did change how you think about it. It won't ever be the same again. When you reframe something for somebody, they can't ever think about it the same way again. Can't go back."

A-ha. Three big ones.

1. The healer did change how I thought about what had been (until that reframe) just a huge and scary pain in the butt.
2. I could not think of it, could not even feel the pain at the time, without connecting to it what Spider's plans for me might be. I wrote the play my brother saw out of Spider's plans. I am writing this book out of Spider's plans. Seven years later, Spider's plans continue to be, for me, an active force in my creative life.
3. I realized that what I was doing sometimes in making Flannery O'Connor's "passages by dragons" was using stories in such a way that the experience recounted would come to have a larger meaning than the original story as it came to me from the community. Some stories were

bigger than others. The drowning story (from the Mennonite community; see the previous chapter) became a lamentation for every parent who ever lost a child, including the biblical King David. Now, that is big and tremendously useful in the making of art with relevance in a community, but sometimes an individual's thinking (or a group's thinking) about themselves or their experience can be changed and that is a different order of magnitude.

I began to study the idea of reframing experience.*

The process of reframing is rather fashionable in some psychology circles, including NLP practitioners who take it as one of their basic commandments. I began to use this learning in my work. Sometimes, stories that are important in a community, stories that a community is still living with no matter how old or how awful the events, come in a collection of stories I am to write from for a play. They are the stories with the flashing neon arrows pointing at them. A story that shows up two or three times, or comes up in conversation more than once while I am in a place indicates that the story has life in that place, and is a story I probably should address.

Simply recounting a painful story just opens old wounds. To be about healing, I need to reframe it. What follows is my reframing of a couple of very hard stories.

The first comes from a small town in Mississippi. The story recounts the murder of a black man by a white man before the civil rights movement took hold there. The black man was a leader, a preacher, in his community. The white man never stood trial, and later was elected sheriff in the county. The project was created for and performed in the county/town where the killing happened and this story was included in the play. I don't know about the church situation at the time of the killing, but now there is an active church on almost every other corner, I have never seen a small town so thoroughly churched, not to mention having an active church at every crossroads in the county. So I did the reframing in a context of Christian religious mythology. I am not changing the story itself. I go to a different frame and something different can happen out of the same events, the irony is that I go to a *really* different frame with this one, the Pearly Gates of Heaven for a confrontation between the dead man and his killer.

A: What I'm fixing to say ain't what the paper said.

B: What did the paper say?

A: You lookin' for what the paper said, you go read the paper.

B: Paper said they had a fight.

A: You know that much, you already read the paper.

B: So I did.

A: Wasn't no fight.

B: Who says?

A *(A silence)*:

B: What kind of witness are you that you won't say your name?

A: A live one.

B *(A silence)*:

A: I'm the same color as the man that's dead, and the fellow that shot him ain't that color and he is still alive. Maybe somebody'll ask about this story and I'll say my name when I tell it; maybe when the man that is still alive dies, I'll tell it at his funeral. Maybe that's how it will work. Maybe I'll be preaching or something that Sunday morning,

B: I didn't know you were a preacher.

A: I'm not. But maybe I'm going to be that Sunday morning, and I'm gonna preach a sermon about how this fellow dies. He's such a fine old fellow, he dies at home in his bed and everybody just cries and cries, and his soul rises up out of his body and heads for Judgment. And he gets on up toward the Pearly Gates, and he sees somebody sitting there outside of them. The Pearly Gates got steps like the courthouse and this fellow sees somebody sitting on the steps up to the Pearly Gates. Gates are closed. He can't see inside of them. And this ain't what he expects, see, he expects the Heavenly Hosts to be out there throwing a welcoming party. Bar-b-que. Fish fry. That's what he done when he run for sheriff. You hear what I said I might preach?

B: Yes. But the paper named Pen Bascome's killer.

A: And this fellow gets up closer and he sees it is a man sitting on the steps, gets a good look at him and recognizes him, says, "Pen Bascome! Well!" This ain't who he expected, ain't who he wanted, but he's gonna make the best of it. "I'm mighty glad to see you. I owe you a big apology. I've been mighty sorry for a long time that gun I was holding went off when it did.

A: And Pen Bascome says, "That gun didn't just go off." And this fellow says, "Well, ok, I shot it, but you were holding that big stick like you were going to hit me with it." And Pen Bascome says, "I didn't have no stick." The fellow says, "We'd been arguing about a tree that was down, who was going to get the boards out of it." And Pen Bascome says, "I don't remember no argument. I don't even remember no tree down. I remember you come onto my property. I remember you didn't like a black man owning property. Didn't want a black man getting ahead." The fellow says, "Pen Bascome, we played together as children, what are you doing sitting here on the steps to the Pearly Gates?" And Pen Bascome says, "That's what you said then, we played together as children; you remember what else you said?" The fellow says, "I probably said something about the good times we had." And Pen Bascome says, "Maybe you should remember a little harder. You said we played together as children and I told you then I was probably going to have to kill you . . ." And then you pulled that gun on me and you shot it. Ran into town yelling about a tree down and how I threatened you in an argument over who got the boards and you killed me in self-defense.

B: That's the story that was in the paper, about the tree and the argument.

A: Listen: This is important. Pen Bascome, he says, "I never threatened you. I never had the chance."

B: You know that to be true?

A: I'm preaching it in my sermon aren't I? And what happens then is that Pen Bascome gets up from where he's sitting, and he turns around and walks up the steps to the Gate, and the Gate opens for him like it knows he's there, and this fellow gets a little peek inside and it looks like the best place he's ever seen. And Pen Bascome stops right in the Gate and turns and says to this fellow, "May the Lord have mercy on your soul." And he goes on through the Gate and the Gate closes behind him and Pen Bascome is gone. And the fellow is standing there looking, wondering what comes next, where's Saint Peter? And the Pearly Gates kind of dissolve in front of him, and there is another set of gates, but they're not near so pretty and what's on the other side is not so pretty either, but these are the gates that open in front of him. This wasn't what he thought would happen at the Judgment. He thought he'd get to explain himself, sit down with Saint Peter and talk man to man, and admit, yes, he done some wrong when he was younger but it was what the South was like and he'd made up for it after the boycott, when he gave a black man a decent job. And Saint Peter would slap him on the back and say he knew about things like that, he'd been a good old boy himself one time, and everything would be fine. Might have to spend a little time in jail in Heaven but this was eternity, what's a few months or even years in eternity? But he hadn't even seen Saint Peter. He'd just seen Pen Bascome, or maybe Pen Bascome was Saint Peter, or was his Saint Peter or something like that. Maybe the people you killed were the ones who sat in Judgment. If that was true, he needed to let his brother know. His brother had killed more folks than he had: DON'T DIE, he needed to tell him. It isn't what you think it is gonna be. All this would be something to think about in the endless time that stretched in front of him in the place that wasn't Heaven.

B: You done with that sermon?

A: I am. Amen.

Now, justice was not done in the place the story came from or, for that matter, in this world. I can't fix that, I can only acknowledge it. What the reframing offers is the possibility of another kind of justice. And just as important, what the black community in that place knows as truth finally got told in a public way.

Here is a second example of a reframing. This is a personal reframing, the turn happens for/with one individual, the mother in the story.

> *(A mother and her daughter are present onstage. The daughter can talk to the audience and her mother; the mother talks only to her daughter. The mother is preparing a plate of food with modern conveniences.)*

DAUGHTER *(To the audience)*: Some wounds don't heal. Not ever, no matter what you do. My mother has a few of those.

MOTHER: Visible scars are important.

DAUGHTER *(To the audience)*: She was very young when her mother died, and her father married again. He married the hardest woman I ever knew. It was years later when I met her, and my mother was a grown woman, married with a daughter of her own. Me.

MOTHER: Hate is a bitter pill, but a big enough dose will keep you alive a long time.

DAUGHTER *(To the audience)*: Mother fixes her food. Carries it a quarter of a mile down the road to her because she can't cook for herself anymore.

MOTHER: Poorhouse won't have her but I can't let her starve. I don't know why, except Jesus tells me to turn the other cheek. When she married Daddy, she knew he had a child, but after she started having children of her own, she didn't want me there. She went crazy. She tried to kill me. More than once.

DAUGHTER *(To her mother)*: That's a terrible thing to say.

MOTHER: It's why the visible scars are important. Proof of what you remember. She was afraid of really doing it, I think, but if it had happened by something she could have called an accident, she wouldn't have been sorry.

DAUGHTER *(To the audience)*: There are things now mother won't do.

MOTHER: I will not handle an ax. I won't look at an ax. I'll clean a chicken and I'll cook it, but don't ask me to cut its head off. Don't ask me to chop wood. I'll saw wood, but I'll not chop it.

DAUGHTER *(To the audience)*: She's been chased with an ax.

MOTHER: And I don't want to have to watch nobody sharpen an ax either.

DAUGHTER *(To the audience)*: She'd had the tips of her fingers cut off with an ax.

MOTHER: She told my father it was an accident but it wasn't, and she and God and I know it.

DAUGHTER *(To her mother)*: There was a woman down the road . . .

MOTHER: I had a friend, a woman old enough to be my mother, who would protect me from her and when she got mad. I'd run down to my friend's house and wait for Daddy to come get me. My stepmother would come beat on that house with her ax. With the handle of it. And threaten me. She beat me with the ax handle sometimes, if she caught me. My friend would tell her to go home if she didn't want the law told on her and to send my father down there when he got home. My friend would tell her she was going to shoot her if she didn't go, was going to sue her if she busted anymore siding off the house, and eventually she'd get over her rage and go along. And later, my father would come down the road and get me, and as long as he was in our house I was safe. She told him lies about what I did and didn't do, and at first he'd get mad at me, but he caught on. It didn't take him long, and after a while he'd just sit stony-faced and stare at her. I was the devil on Earth according to her but he knew better. He had to get in bed with that woman at night and wonder what on earth he had done.

DAUGHTER *(To her mother, from here on)*: Mama, that's funny. Laying there wide awake in the bed at night wondering what in God's name had come over him when he married her.

MOTHER: Funny? I reckon it's funny. I didn't spend much time laughing about it.

DAUGHTER: Of course not then. Laugh now.

MOTHER *(A snort)*: I know what he did. By then, he had other children to protect.

DAUGHTER: Well, at least you weren't there during school.

MOTHER: There's some more to the story. I didn't get to go to school much.

DAUGHTER: Why not?

MOTHER: Well, my father worked a job, and when my stepmother got pregnant, she was sick all the time and somebody had to keep our garden and the cotton we planted, and that somebody was me.

DAUGHTER: So you're there all day.

MOTHER: I'd get up before daylight and go to work with no breakfast, or just what I could run out of the house with, so I wouldn't be alone with her. I worked from the time I was eight, but sometimes I just couldn't stay out of her way, and I'd end up down at our neighbor's house until Daddy got home. But one afternoon, my friend wasn't there. The house was open, everybody left their doors unlocked then, and I ran in, my stepmother coming behind me, but my friend wasn't there, nobody was, and my stepmother realized I was alone and came in the house after me. I ran out the back door and headed towards home. I needed a place to get around things or under something I guess. I don't know why I headed home, but I did, and she was . . . she had that ax. She always had that damn ax.

DAUGHTER: Mother, if it wasn't so awful, that would be almost funny too, like something from the Saturday morning cartoons, like Wile E. Coyote . . .

MOTHER: I climbed a tree in our yard because I didn't think she could do that.

DAUGHTER: And she couldn't?

MOTHER *(Still preparing food)*: She didn't even try. She was pregnant and sick. She whacked it a couple of times. I guess she decided that was too much work, cutting it down. So she got straw from the shed and branches of kindling wood, and she lit a fire around the bottom of the tree.

DAUGHTER: Oh, Mother . . . a big fire?

MOTHER: Big enough. My legs were burnt. My arms were burnt. I got the scars. The clothes where I wasn't pressed against the tree were scorched stiff.

DAUGHTER: What did she do?

MOTHER: She watched. I knew I was dead if the tree caught fire, but I knew I was dead if I went down, too, so I just sort of held on. I held on till Daddy got home. The tree saved my life. Daddy had to come up it to get me, I couldn't let go. He carried me down out of it over one hip like you might carry a calf. He was trying not to touch places that were burned. He carried me into the shed and laid me down and put sewing machine oil on my burns. He didn't even ask what had happened. He was crying.

I wasn't. I was dried out of tears. He took me down to my friend's house and we waited till she got back home, and he asked if I could stay there for a while, said he'd bring the extra food for me and pay for my keep, said my stepmother would not come down there ever again, he'd see to it, he'd kill her if she did. And my friend took me in. I didn't go back home. If I wanted to see my daddy, I went out to his job. We ate a lot of lunches together. After a couple of years, I hired out to other people for my keep, and then I married young. That day, my friend washed the oil off of me and brewed fever grass and washed my burns with it, said the fever grass would take the fire out of them and it did. The burns healed.

(The mother finishes preparing the food.)

DAUGHTER: Why do you do this?

MOTHER: Her own children won't have anything to do with her.

DAUGHTER: That's not a reason, Mother . . .

MOTHER: It is true that I think of that tree and the fire every time I fix her a plate of food. It happened and I lived though it. But, see, I don't mind if she thinks of it too while she eats the food I fix for her. And she has to eat that food every day to stay alive.

(The mother crosses the stage with the food and leaves it on a table, and calls to someone we never see.)

Come on, old woman, get your supper while it's hot . . .

The reframing in this piece is a little more subtle, it happens in the last couple of lines spoken by the mother. The real woman, the woman whose story it is, had not considered what it might cost her stepmother to eat the food she fixed. She had only lived with what it cost her to fix it. It had cost a lot. It was a difficult duty in the story as it came to me. With the reframing, she can see this duty in a different way. First, it was a duty she had chosen to do, and second, who knows what hell it cost the old woman to eat the food she fixed? She could almost enjoy the duty she had chosen: sweet potatoes as sweet revenge. Uncomfortable, isn't it? It will be much easier to live with such a story when that sweet potato is just another sweet potato, and the woman herself can come to something other than revenge. But revenge is a step out of years of being a victim, and any step away from seeing herself as a victim is a step in a useful direction.

Now, the ethics of this reframing business can get tricky.** Who am I to assume the right to reframe stories in which anger/pain is, to say the least, justified? Some squirrelly middle-aged white lady with barely enough knowledge about something to be messing with it. How do I assume the right to use such knowledge? I don't know, but the Dalai Lama tells us the human job of this world is finding/creating happiness, and a little arrogant artistry goes a long way.***

From the energy work, I do know that for the short-term health of a human being, anger is often very useful. It can be a survival strategy. That is what it is supposed to be, but if it is held long-term, it is toxic. It does literal damage to the organism. So any anger or pain I can help release with the reframing of any story is, at the very least, a gesture toward well-being in the body (bodies) to whom the story matters.

⊰ THE ASTERISKS ⊱

*My NLP consultant brother argues this point. He says I did do a reframing in the Mennonite's drowning story because I managed to turn a story of such loss into a lament with a wider application. I think I made a good dragon passage for that story when the surviving son, his mother who is telling the story onstage, and the audience all realize that that young man had to quit fighting the things he thought were killing him and agree to die to find he could walk to shore and live. I gave the story no new meaning or possibility: that is what really happened. It was a real dragon passage in real life; I just pointed out the passage and clarified it in the way I wrote the scene for stage. Now, that story may have gotten reframed in the community because of our use of it, stories really do have their own lives sometimes, but I did not do a reframing in the writing of it.

Reframing is not a complex idea, but I'm actually using it in more than one aspect in this book so allow me to elaborate a little . . . When Pen Bascome's murder story is told as a confrontation between Pen Bascome and the man who murdered him on the steps to the Pearly Gates of Heaven, it is obviously not something that happened in this world but a new level of truth telling is possible, so it is a reframing of that story. Now, this reframing has no value for Pen Bascome, he's already dead, but it does have value for people who knew and lived those years with the suppressed version of the story. The reframing was a way to make it public. By setting the scene out of this world—moving quite literally to a new frame, all puns intended—I opened the story to be told in an emotionally satisfactory and dramatically interesting way. This was a truly theatrical application of the idea of reframing a story.

The burn story is a little different. Though what you've read was also a scene written (from a person's real story) for the theater, it illustrates a far more common use of the reframing of stories. In the scene, the woman who was burned is very much alive but, with what I wrote for her, she is no longer just a victim of her stepmother's abuse and ongoing need. She has found a way to change her thinking about her duty; it is now a kind of revenge. This is a reframing of her thinking. It doesn't change her situation; it does change her thinking about her situation. (This kind of reframing was what the shaman did for me with the spider bite: he didn't change my situation, he just changed my thinking about it.) The burn woman can see her ongoing duty a new way because of the reframing. Now, this particular reframing is uncomfortable. We might be happier with her if she came to some sort of compassion for the old woman, if it were a compassionate potato she delivered to the old woman's door.

But consider this: we don't know how the stepmother feels about the food she eats. We make assumptions from what we hear her stepdaughter say. We never see or hear from the stepmother. A potato of compassion could be even harder for her to swallow than her stepdaughter's anger. Perhaps these two have fallen to the only situation that can keep them both alive. But they are both alive, and life ongoing always suggests a possibility of further change . . .

Now, I just did another reframing of this story for you, the reader, when I gave you a different way to think about what the stepmother might feel and what might come next between these two in this story.

⊰ ⊱

**The ethics of writing at all is tricky because writing is a predatory business. My aunt Sally used to introduce me by saying, "Be careful what you say to her, she'll use it!" I told her she blew my cover with that line, and she laughed like she was supposed to, but she never would quit saying it. There was a way in which she was proud of me, but there was another way in which she really was warning her friends. She had a point. I mine experience like Peabody mines coal, my own and others' experience, and I'm pretty indiscriminate. Everything is potential material.

We have to consume life to live it (I learned that first from Joseph Campbell). My politically correct organic tomato soup was once live tomatoes, and I kid myself if I think I'm not consuming life when I slurp that soup. The hunger for stories is not a body hunger (like the hunger for tomato soup), but it is a huge and fierce hunger, and it is as necessary for human well-being as food is for the body. We have to make stories and we have to consume stories or our brains don't work right, and when we consume stories, we are consuming life. Stories carry energy, they make patterns in the way we think and behave, and we have to have them to live in a social order.

Maybe some of us are more hungry for stories than others, and maybe those with the greatest hunger are the ones who become the dealers in stories. For me, the hunger is great enough that my own heart and any one else's are fair game. I come to the writing business with something akin to the ethics of a goshawk.

I live in a social order, so I do try to honor privacy in the stories I use with the community work, and I credit where credit is due. For myself, I care that the stories I use have heat and heart, whatever those indefinable things are. William Faulkner's "old verities" (language from his Nobel acceptance speech) is a description of "heat and heart," though I doubt that all of Mr. Faulkner's verities and mine are the same because of the difference in our times and our sexes. They shouldn't be the same. Experience is not the same, and what is known for truth changes. It has to.

⊰ ⊱

***Comedy. To speak of truly arrogant artistry, there are situations in which the best reframe I can make is to give something a comic context. This is sometimes a rather odd take on what comedy is and does. And, by extension, the tragic. What if Oedipus had said: "Aw, shit!" and done something more useful than gouging his eyes out? Or Lear: "You like your meat salty, lady, but pass me the gravy . . ." I know, I'm doing violence to tragic tradition. I do understand that the making of tragedy is the character flaw, the hubris, that doesn't allow Oedipus to consider his situation as nothing more than a revolting development. Or Lear to understand what his daughter is saying about love. This is an interesting way to think.

Comedy is about survival. Find some way to laugh, or die. The tragic is about the inability to find the absurd in a situation and the resultant inability to laugh at it. That obviously doesn't mean comedy is always light or easy. Comedy can be truly brutal, maybe more brutal in some ways than the tragic (which honors the character flaw). The hard ironic comedy that makes you laugh and cry at the same time is dangerous stuff.

Now, I understand that terrible things happen in the world, people sometimes die of things they shouldn't have to die of, and people leave holes in other people's lives. I know that loss and grief and anger and fear are real, and I do not mean to make light of any of those circumstances. But I also know there are more and less productive ways to live or die of them, and the comedic turn is almost always the one that points toward further life.

This is another reframing job, and it is another hard story, but this one took a comic turn in the reframe. It is a return to the front steps of the Pearly Gates. (I do seem to need to go there sometimes.) I'm taking my permission—that arrogant artistry—for these Pearly Gates reframings from *The Tibetan Book of the Dead*. The teaching says (I'm simplifying) that we carry some of our failings from this life beyond death (these determine our next reincarnation), and that in the time immediately following death—the time between when we die and when we are reincarnated (the bardos)—we get at least some of the experience we expect and think we deserve at the time we die. In the two Pearly Gates reframings I discuss here, the killer is obliged to confront the person or persons he killed.

In this story, two black women were robbed and murdered by a white man. The man was caught because one of the murdered women, Bernice, had developed the habit of writing her name on the money she earned, and he had her autographed money in his mouth when he was caught. He was trying to hide it and he didn't think the sheriff would look in his mouth. It was actually a "law and order" story in the community. It was told about a sheriff who refused to hang a white man for killing two black women. A deputy stepped up and did the job. As I used the story, the murder and eventual hanging unfolded over the course of the play *Crooked Rivers: Sisters Three*. We saw Bernice learn to read and write, so we know why she signs the money she earns, we saw the two women get shot, we saw the murderer get caught, and we saw the sheriff refuse to do his job and his deputy agree to do it. This reframe is in the last scene of the play.

> *(Bernice and Carol Ann are sitting on the front steps of the Pearly Gates. Over to one side is a second gate. For the first gate, something simple that says PEARLY GATES and opens and closes is fine, we don't need an elaborate representation of what the Pearly Gates might be. Or of what the gates of hell might look like either, that sign simply says OTHER GATE. Both sets of gates need to open and close.)*

BERNICE: I'm about ready to go back in, I like it a whole lot better inside these gates than out here, inside these gates is Heaven!

CAROL ANN: A-men, sister. Inside these Gates . . .

BERNICE: Well, it was you run all over Heaven this morning trying to figure if we needed to be here noon daylight savings or real noon, and then it was you insisted we come out here what everybody in there figured was an hour early . . .

CAROL ANN: A note like that comes around for you, sister, you get it right . . .

BERNICE: Oh, I agree. A note like that comes around and you *want* to do what it says. I'm sitting here, aren't I?

CAROL ANN: My note said there'd be something I'd want to see passing by the Pearly Gates just after noon.

BERNICE: Mine, too. Said I probably need to give some directions.

CAROL ANN: Mine, too . . .

BERNICE: What kind of directions you figure that might be?

CAROL ANN: I don't know. You step inside the Pearly Gates and it is clearer than daylight where you are but out here, well, there's these gates and those gates . . .

BERNICE: But then you got worried that might be daylight savings noon and we've been sitting out here . . .

CAROL ANN: I'm sorry about the time stuff . . .

BERNICE: You know something? You don't have to be sorry. I got all the time in Heaven.

(They are comfortable.)

BERNICE: These blessed steps don't even hurt to lay back on . . .

CAROL ANN: Hey. Look yonder.

(Their murderer with his neck at an odd angle approaches, they watch him come.)

CAROL ANN: You know this fellow?

BERNICE: I believe I do.

CAROL ANN: Me, too. His neck sure looks funny.

(He approaches, ignores them.)

MAN *(Calls)*: Saint Peter! Saint Peter!

(Nothing happens, he steps up to the Gates and cannot open them. Then he notices the women.)

One of you go fetch Saint Peter for me.

BERNICE: Do what?

MAN: There's been a mistake and I need to see Saint Peter.

BERNICE: Saint Peter, he's a busy man . . .

MAN: No back talk, just hop to.

BERNICE: Do I look like a bunny to you?

CAROL ANN: What kind of mistake you think you made?

MAN: I been hung, dammit, ain't my mistake.

CAROL ANN: Well, whose mistake was it?

MAN: Look, they said I murdered these two . . . .

CAROL ANN: Did you?

MAN: Well, both those women died but it wasn't intentional.

CAROL ANN: I see. I had some experience with dying by surprise myself.

BERNICE: Both us have.

MAN: You shoot somebody?

BERNICE: Nope. Got shot. Both of us. And here we are.

CAROL ANN: Experience is experience.

MAN: I just happened to shoot one woman, it was an accident, I wasn't trying to murder anybody, I just needed some money, and the other saw me do it and I couldn't have any witnesses . . . I figure I need to speak with Saint Peter. I need to be able to explain myself before he passes Judgment . . .

BERNICE: What else you got in your mouth besides a twisted tongue?

MAN: You calling me a liar?

[He is lying, and people watching the play know it.]

BERNICE: You know when you were on Earth and they said put your money where your mouth is, they didn't mean put the money in your mouth.

CAROL ANN: They especially didn't mean put somebody else's money in your mouth.

MAN: Look. I'm talking funny 'cause my neck is broke. I just been hung. There isn't any money in my mouth.

CAROL ANN: Now.

MAN: Get up from there and go fetch Saint Peter.

BERNICE: I think that might be Mr. Saint Peter in this circumstance.

MAN: Him and me got some negotiating to do.

BERNICE: What you got to negotiate?

MAN: What it going to take for me to get into Heaven. Now get your sorry rear end up from there and go fetch Pete like I told you to.

(A pause in which nobody moves.)

CAROL ANN: I think I'm feeling a direction, how about you?

BERNICE: Yep. I'm feeling it, too. No question.

MAN: I don't care what you feel, just do what I told you to!

CAROL ANN: Can't. This here is the back gate.

MAN: What do you mean "the back gate"?

BERNICE: Heaven got two gates. This one plenty fine-looking, but it is the back gate.

CAROL ANN: Sure is.

MAN: Ah, yes. I should have known. You two wouldn't be sitting out front, would you . . .

CAROL ANN: That's what you're thinking.

BERNICE: And Saint Peter, he doesn't meet folks out the back gate, see. You got to go around the other side.

Maybe get in line. He's got a lot of business right now what with the state of the world, he's awful busy looking stuff up in that big book . . .

MAN: What book?

CAROL ANN: Big heavy book. I've not read it.

MAN: I'd be most surprised if you had.

CAROL ANN: You know, a nice little note–that's words written on paper for a person to read–a little note from Saint Peter come around this morning, signed "Your Brother in Heaven, Saint Peter." One come to each of us. Special delivery. Cutest little angel runs the special delivery. Said, there'd be somebody out here right about now needing directions. Said, would we please come out here and wait for them and tell them what they need to know. Said, it works that way up here sometimes.

MAN: Saint Peter sent you?

CAROL ANN: Certainly did. Sent us.

MAN: Sent you two to give *me* directions.

BERNICE: Seems to be the situation.

MAN: Well, at least Saint Peter was aware of my impending arrival . . .

BERNICE: He usually is.

CAROL ANN: And your direction is to go around front.

MAN: And how do I get around front?

CAROL ANN: You see *that* gate?

MAN: That don't look like the gate I want.

BERNICE: How you know what you are looking for? You just got here.

CAROL ANN: You go through that gate.

BERNICE: And you gon' walk for a long time. How's your shoe leather?

MAN: Shoe leather?

BERNICE: Your sole.

CAROL ANN: It'll seem like an eternity, but Heaven is a big place, really big, and you got to go around, got to get all the way up to the other gate.

MAN: That gate leads to it?

CAROL ANN: That gate.

MAN: I really don't think that's the gate I want.

BERNICE: Saint Peter, he may start wondering where you got to, might forget you if you're not careful, and you got a ways to go.

CAROL ANN: Time's a wastin', man.

MAN: You're sure.

CAROL ANN: Never been more sure of anything.

BERNICE: Do it.

(So the man exits through the Other Gate.)

BERNICE *(After him)*: What I really meant was, "Hop to it."

CAROL ANN: You figure Heaven's got a back gate?

BERNICE: Not that I know of.

CAROL ANN: So you figure he'll walk all the way around.

BERNICE: I don't know where all he will have to walk, but I'll tell you something: if that same man gets back here, and if Saint Peter sends me out here a second time to give directions, and that man is still talking about how SOMEBODY ELSE made a big mistake, I will tell him he missed the turnoff first time around, and that he has to go back, and I will send him through that other gate all over again.

CAROL ANN: And if he says he made a mistake?

BERNICE: I will take him to Saint Peter and plead his case myself.

CAROL ANN: I'm proud to know you, sister. You ready?

BERNICE: I am.

(They exit through the Pearly Gates.)

The reframing here, another situation in which the murdered get to confront their killer, is also dependent on *The Tibetan Book of the Dead* teaching (that we carry some of the failures of this life with us, and that we get at least some of what we expect in the time immediately after death) for validity. So if this man is hung with his prejudices intact, still thinking his own life more valuable than the two he took, meeting the two women he killed is not beyond the realm of *Tibetan Book of the Dead* possibility. Except I don't think you have to know the Tibetan teaching for Bernice and Carol Ann and their killer's situation (and Bernice and Carol Ann's surprising grace in it) to have an emotional impact. But who is the reframe for? All these people are already dead, and the community already knew the story. This one is for the audience that saw the play. They've seen Bernice and Carol Ann murdered earlier in the play, and to find Bernice and Carol Ann again in the final scene is a wondrous shock of the kind that can only happen in the theater, and it offers a possibility they (probably) never thought about before. Obviously, I have no real idea about how such a confrontation might work or even if it could. I've never been to the Pearly Gates myself, but for the Pen Bascome story and for this one and for the business of making plays, the imaginative trip to the Pearly Gates offers a confrontation (and maybe a measure of justice) that was simply not available in this world, and that is a reframing.

Further Practice

MY PEARLY GATES PERMISSION

Thurman, Robert (translator), introduction by Huston Smith. *The Tibetan Book of the Dead*. New York: Bantam Books, 1994.

This is an ancient book, pretty close to unreadable in most translations, but Thurman has done a good job of making sense of it.

ABOUT NLP REFRAMING

Bandler, Richard and John Grinder. *Reframing: Neurolinguistic Programming and the Transformation of Meaning*, Moab, UT: Real People Press, 1982.

This is a foundation book for neurolinguistic programming.

The Stories

The Pen Bascome story was told by the murdered man's son, collected by David and Patricia Crosby, and published in a small magazine called *I Ain't Lying,* by Mississippi Cultural Crossroads in Port Gibson, Mississippi. I have changed the murdered man's name for this book. I also heard the story from other sources when I was in Port Gibson. Mississippi Cultural Crossroads, the organization for which I wrote the play *The Deal Rocked Up,* is headed by Patricia Crosby with considerable community support and does a number of things in and for the community, including a summer theater for young people directed by David Crosby. MCC's website—msculturalcrossroads.org—is absolutely worth a visit. They sell incredible quilts, bed quilts and art quilts, handmade at MCC by local quilters. It is a great way to spend your money . . .

The Burn story was told to Joy Jinks for the Swamp Gravy project in Colquitt, Georgia. I did not use a name in the story as it was onstage, either.

The Money in the Mouth story came from Southeast Georgia's, Crooked Rivers Project and was written for *Crooked Rivers: Sisters Three.* I heard the story from several sources when I was there. These names are also changed.

THE PHYSICAL KEEPING OF EMOTION IN THE BODY

CANDACE PERT, PH.D., discovered in the 1970s (and wrote about in *Molecules of Emotion*) that our brains–maybe better said, our minds because our minds are no longer considered to be just the gray matter in our heads–our minds make specific chemicals that are released into our bodies depending on the different emotions we experience. She called these chemicals neuropeptides. These chemicals come into being with connectors literally built into them, and almost all the cells in our bodies have receptors for these connectors. Neuropeptides join the cells in our bodies when we experience emotion. Imagine organic snaps. Each new emotion brings another wash of neuropeptides. Neuropeptides change our body's chemistry with our emotions (a person's tears of joy and the same person's tears of grief are literally not the same chemically), and our cells evolve to become more receptive to the specific neuropeptides they are most accustomed to. If you spend a lot of time angry, your body makes more receptors in its cells for the angry chemicals, and you will be even more disposed to anger. The hard emotions we feel (like anger or grief) must be dealt with and let go before the chemistry in our body changes again. Some neuropeptides are better for us than others;

some, like those associated with anger or fear, have tremendous short-term survival value but can be hard on the body if they are held long-term. The love-joy based emotions and their related chemicals are good for the body. That is a very, very simplified statement of the science.

Since she published her revolutionary *Molecules* book, Dr. Pert has gone even further. She says, "Your body is your subconscious mind." What she is saying with that statement is that your experience is literally held in your body, and your body is literally part of your mind. This is a huge idea.

In energy work, for example the practice of shiatsu, the practitioner's job is to find those places in the body where old emotions are held and, through finger pressure, to release them. This is hard to believe until you see someone (or experience it yourself) break into tears with a very specific memory from some finger pressure on their back or shoulders. A good shiatsu practitioner can literally feel the places that need work. Often, it is not so specific as one single spot per memory or event, but occasionally it is. The places where we hold things are rather predictable. There seem to be emotional storage bins particularly in the muscles of the upper back and shoulders, and the thighs and calves, but every cell in the body has receptors for neuropeptides. Shiatsu was what demonstrated to me that an old experience can be literally held in the body. (The spider story in the Introduction of this book recounts the moment when my shaman friend, pressing on my back, made me cry with very, very specific memories.) Shiatsu can help with the release of old emotion (a technique called Rolfing sets out to do the same thing with deep muscle work), but unless we learn to think in a different way about the experience that caused that particular collection of neuropeptides (or whatever else it is that is held in the tissue—something is held, it is just very hard to name exactly what), those places of held experience return to our bodies.

Further evidence* that the events of our lives are literally held in the tissues of our bodies comes from heart-and-organ-transplant patients in which the recipient of a heart or a lung from a dead donor will remember things (or feelings) that happened to the dead donor. The most astonishing of these stories is one of a child who remembered her donor's murder. (This story is recounted in the introduction of *The Heart's Code*, listed in Further Practice.) With what the police already knew added to her new heart's knowledge, the murderer was caught. It was a knowledge that came with a lot of terror (emotion) when the murdered donor's heart was transplanted and beating in the recipient's body.

When I provide a good passage by a dragon, or when I reframe a story so an individual can no longer think the same way about an experience, I am also working on those places in the body where memory is held, releasing old chemistry, installing new. I am changing the chemistry of the individual(s) to whom the story matters. If I reframe a story so that painful experience comes to have some value or resolution, I am not just stopping the production of those old neuropeptides held around that event, I am causing different ones to circulate in the individual body or bodies.

We seem to be designed to learn from and let go of emotions that are fear-based (anger, grief, fear, all those) and to bathe ourselves regularly in the love-joy based ones. The happier emotions do really good things in our bodies. They improve immune-system functioning, we are literally physically stronger when we are happy, we have more energy . . . this list goes on. But the neuropeptides created by love-joy emotions don't seem to settle in quite the same way that harder emotions do. We are, by our design, supposed to let go of hard stuff and learn to live in love. This is straight Buddhist teaching. The words of Christ can be read as how-to instructions.

There is a whole branch of popular psychology—look at the self-help shelf of any bookstore—that is about letting go of old hurts and coming to forgiveness. The major premise of this work is that the act of forgiveness is not for the transgressor, it does nothing one way or the other for the transgressor. The transgressor has his or her own debts to pay. Coming to forgiveness has value for the person who suffered the transgression and manages to let go of it. There is a tricky but important line to draw here. Forgiveness is not saying to the transgressor, imaginatively or really, "What you did was ok." That is often simply not true, and to force someone to say or try to feel that is to take away agency from the transgressed, and that is never a good idea.

Miguel Ruiz, a teacher in the Toltec (energy) tradition, wrote a book called *The Four Agreements*. The second of those agreements suggests you learn not to take anything personally to begin with. He says that what others say or do is a projection of their own reality, their own "dream," and if you can understand that, you won't be such a victim of suffering due to someone else's actions. That is a tremendously useful way to think. It is a variation of forgiveness, just not what we usually think about when we use the word.

The thing to understand about coming to forgiveness is that it is also about creating a different set of neuropeptides in our bodies. One of the how-to ideas in the coming-to-forgiveness counseling practiced these days is to find the value in painful events, in other words, to provide a dragon passage for them or to reframe them for ourselves or with the help of a counselor. It often takes a counselor or some other outside ear to do it.

In short, our bodies mirror any and every mental event we experience, there is chemistry that literally affects health and well-being connected to how we perceive the events of our minutes, our days, and our lives, and if you change the perception of events, you change the chemistry.**

⊰ The Asterisks ⊱

*Body memory: Deepak Chopra explains (and biology concurs) that our bodies change cells all the time, our skin is new every month or so, our liver is new every six weeks, in every portion of our bodies cells die and are replaced by new ones, even some in the brain. DNA does not change, so we still look like we used to, but we are literally not made of the same matter that we were a year ago. Here is the trip: our memory is more permanent than our matter. Chopra says your body is the place your memory calls home. So what is a cell? It is a memory that has collected some matter around itself.

⊰ ⊱

**Changing bodies: You can do more than just change chemistry when you change thinking. The body whose chemistry is changed can prove to be its own revelation. I've been collecting "knock of the spirit" stories (I explain "knock of the spirit" in the chapter called "Shamanic Soul Retrieval and a Digression About 'The Knock of the Spirit,'" but briefly, a knock of the spirit is something you can't ignore for whatever reasons) and one of them follows here. This is not a story from one of the community plays. I'm still watching this one unfold. But it is a reframing story and a body that is changing—at least in part—for the reframing.

A friend, seven years ago, quit her job because of pain she was feeling, and was diagnosed by her doctor with fibromyalgia. I tell this story with her permission.

Shortly after the diagnosis, she had a car wreck in which she was literally scalped (her scalp was sewn back on in the ER), she damaged three vertebrae in her neck, and had an out-of-body experience. She was outside the car looking back at herself, and she decided that if she didn't live through it, that was ok, but if she was going to live through it, she needed to get back in her body, so she did. Back in her body and back in the wreck, she had lost the ability to move by herself and lost the ability to talk.

A couple of years of physical therapy followed. Some small capacity to walk returned, very labored, with a walker, but no regaining of speech at all.

Her physical therapist, a year and a half into treatment, learned Reiki, and started using it on her. She told my friend there was something else going on, she could feel it. So my friend went back to her doctor and came away this time with a Parkinson's diagnosis. The therapist felt there wasn't anything more she could do with physical therapy, but suggested that my friend try more Reiki.

So two years after her wreck, I met this woman at the same Reiki group I went to for help with the spider bite. She'd been coming to the group for about six months before I showed up. She walked slowly using a cane. She couldn't turn her neck, and she couldn't talk at all. But she had come to this mobility with the Reiki, the Reiki helped, and she soon became a practitioner herself, and a very good one.

Most people who find Reiki want to be able do it, and she was no different.

A very labored speech began to return.

And her friends in the energy community realized she was a little different from the rest of us beginners. As a Reiki practitioner, she could put a tremendous amount of energy through her hands, her hands felt electric, and we began to call her a shaman in training, we talked about the wounded-healer tradition, about how some who come to energy healing are obliged to face their mortality somehow first, and many have some life-changing sickness or accident before they come to their capacity as healers. Many "knock of the spirit" stories begin with an out-of-body experience of some kind. She really did fit a pattern, an archetype. We talked about the silence used in many enlightenment traditions, and she'd certainly been through some enforced silence, more than two years of it. We essentially reframed—without thinking about it that way, we were just watching and trying to name the astonishing changes we were seeing—the last few years of her experience.

She says the reframing of her situation—when people spoke of the wounded healer archetype as it might apply to her, and then the learning through the time in which she literally became something of a wounded healer—was as life-changing as the car wreck itself. It made some sense out of very, very hard experience, it gave her permission to explore the new abilities she was finding in herself, even in the face of an abusive husband and disapproving family.

The process is still unfolding, the bottom line not yet lived, but her speech is now normal unless she is tired, and then she slows down a little. She walks better now than she did before the car wreck, no cane at all. The diagnosed Parkinson's condition has improved, she's taking less medicine for it than she was at first, and the fibromyalgia seems to be gone. (The fibromyalgia—current medical thinking in this case—was probably misdiagnosed

Parkinson's.) She is as swivel-headed as the rest of us. The neck that didn't work for three years after the wreck now works like it is supposed to. Her face is no longer mask-like. It was when I first met her, and for some time afterward, say four years after the wreck. Now, all the muscles move with expression again.

She's gotten a divorce. In energy terms, she acted with intent on her own behalf. She's assumed her own agency. And she becomes a stronger healing practitioner every day.

Another changing-body story is of a woman who was overweight and very shy. I tell this story with her permission. She wouldn't talk much at all for the first several years I knew her. She was stuck in an unhappy marriage, and sleep-deprived because of his horrendous snoring. (When I spent a night as a guest in the house, I was several rooms and closed doors away, very hard-of-hearing myself, and I couldn't sleep because of the snoring.)

She contributed a story of childhood abuse to one of the community plays I was working on. I used it. It was a hard story, but it fit a need in the script and I reframed it in a very odd and, what felt at the time, dangerous way. I did not understand the idea of reframing then, but it was what I did in making a passage by the dragon. I decided to give the abused child some responsibility: the child would make some choices. It was an element in the story the woman told, but I made the child truly capable of making a choice. During the time of the abuse (early 1950s), she had collected a quarter every time she sat on her abuser's lap and allowed him to touch her. She didn't like it at all, but she wanted the quarter.

Whether it was a wise choice or not is patently evident: doing anything that makes you despise yourself is a bad choice, and she hated that she wanted (or needed, needed is a legitimate description) the quarters at all. She despised herself for wanting the money, and she hated the old man. She was jubilant when he died, she was free of him, but there was no question that as a child, she had been capable of making a choice for a quarter and acting on it.

The child's choice for the quarters (she earned them) was implied in the story the woman told. I made the choice evident in the piece I wrote, and I gave full value to the quarters she earned. She was from a poor family and, at that time, a quarter was a loaf of bread.

The next time I saw this woman, about a year and a half after we did that story, she'd divorced her husband (the final straw was that he'd lost some of their property in a poker game). She'd lost a lot of weight. She'd taken to wearing fancy cowboy boots and she talked a blue streak. And she wanted good parts in all the plays.

She was transformed. I have never seen a human being so different from one time to the next. Plastic surgery could not have changed a person as much as this woman had changed—what had changed was so much more than just surface stuff, though that had changed, too. She walked through a door now instead of hanging on the other side of it. She assumed her right to participate in conversation instead of waiting to be encouraged by others to say anything. She had changed how she thought about herself. She had learned to value herself. More, she is now a person capable of making choices and acting on them.

Now, I'm in no position to make judgments about someone else's wise or unwise choices (you wouldn't have caught me dead in those cowboy boots, I want the really pointy-toed ones), and to say that the reframing was what led to all the change is foolishly presumptuous. Just telling that story was tremendously important; we are human, we need witnesses to our experience. Lives can be warped in secret-keeping. Getting out of a marriage that had been feeding her misery for years was equally important. When we did that story, the timing was right for that human being to find something other than a victim in herself, and the reframing of a story from one in which she had seen herself as a victim to one in which she made choices, even if they weren't very good choices—they were a child's choices—was a revelation.

Further Practice

ABOUT FORGIVENESS

Ruiz, M.D., Miguel. *The Four Agreements: A Practical Guide to Personal Freedom*. San Rafael, CA: Amber-Allen Publishing, 1997.

I practice Ruiz's agreements.

ABOUT MIND-BODY CONNECTIONS

Chopra, M.D., Deepak. *Quantum Healing: Exploring the Frontiers of Mind/Body Medicine*. New York: Bantam Books, 1989.

I'm not the biggest fan of Chopra's. I like what he says, but it feels like he says the same thing over and over under his many different book titles. It is, I suppose, one way to sell a lot of books. More power to him. I do recommend this one.

Pearsall, M.D., Paul. *The Heart's Code: Tapping the Wisdom and Power of Our Heart Energy*. New York: Broadway Books, 1998.

The child heart-donor story is told in the introduction to this book.

Pert, Ph.D., Candace. "Your Body Is Your Subconscious Mind," audio CD. Boulder, CO: Sounds True, 2004.

This is a talk that Pert gave (you see what it is about by the title). It includes the Q&A with her audience.

ABOUT NEUROPEPTIDES

Pert, Ph.D., Candace. *Molecules of Emotion: The Science Behind Mind-Body Medicine*. New York: Scribner, 1997.

This is a must-read mind-body book.

The Energy of the Body

ALBERT EINSTEIN did a very large reframe job on Isaac Newton's universe when he said everything is potential energy. The quantum guys couldn't agree more, but they've gone way beyond what Einstein understood, and have done some major universe reframing themselves.

One way to think about the energy business is to begin with the electromagnetic spectrum, which describes a "family" of energy we are capable of measuring by its radiation, including (according to *The American Heritage Dictionary*) cosmic-ray photons, gamma rays, X-rays, ultraviolet radiation, visible light, infrared radiation, microwaves, radio waves, heat and electric currents. What is interesting about this list is that it is open-ended on both ends. These are the things we can perceive (mostly with instruments) and measure and name, but years ago, this list was not nearly as long as it is now, because we had no way to perceive energies like cosmic ray photons, gamma rays, microwaves, radio waves, etc. To state the obvious, just because we cannot yet measure something doesn't mean it doesn't exist. And nobody claims this is the whole of the electromagnetic spectrum. It is a description of what we can know and measure now.

Imagine the book you hold in your hands to be "measurable" in terms of energy. The book is measurable, actually $E=MC^2$ will do the trick: energy equals mass times the speed of light squared. The numbers in this equation get really big, really fast. There is a lot of potential energy in this book. Nuclear physics is, in small part, about converting matter to energy, suddenly in a bomb, in a controlled way in a reactor. (And far less matter than is contained in this book is needed to make a rather large bomb. Don't worry, the book is made of stable elements, it is the ideas that are explosive; a bomb is made with unstable elements and 100% provable ideas.) This matter-to-energy conversion can be measured along the electromagnetic spectrum.

And then, imagine the energy that the energy-healing tradition speaks of as higher than we can currently measure on the open-ended electromagnetic spectrum, or maybe tucked in ("enfolded" is the usual term) in some way we haven't yet understood somewhere along it.

Or, if the enfolding business in the electromagnetic spectrum doesn't suit you, there are the energies we know about that don't seem to fall in the electromagnetic spectrum at all, at least not in a way we understand it. Gravity is one of these, and what quantum physics calls weak and strong atomic forces are others; so if you prefer, this "ki," the energy healers speak of, is another of these energies.

Or if you prefer, "ki" (also "qi," the Japanese term) or "chi" (also "ch'i," Chinese) or "prana" (Indian) is none of these kinds of energies, but you cannot prefer that it just go away. Describable (definable) or not, its effects can be measured. We know of this energy in the same way we are able to perceive gravity and weak atomic force, not by measuring them directly, but by measuring their effects.

The energy-healing community tells us that we are spiritual beings having a physical experience. It is saying we, too, are energy—and we are (that and more). Eastern traditions like Buddhism or Zen, shamanic traditions, and the energy-healer traditions will tell you that not only are we energy, we are sentient energy. They tell you that everything is sentient energy, that the world is sentient, that energy itself is sentient.

Quantum physics is coming closer and closer to the same idea. Most physicists don't go all the way to "sentient" yet (some do), but there does seem to be a web or ground of energy (an "endless field of oscillating possibilities" is one description) of which the universe is made, and in which everything is literally connected somehow to everything else. Connected at speeds faster than the fastest thing we know which is light which travels at 187,000 miles per second. Events in this field happen faster than light. Instantaneous. Faster than instantaneous. Time and distance, in fact the whole of space, don't make any difference at all.

Energy healers tell us that ki is a manifestation of this field of possibilities, this web of energy in which everything is connected. They tell us that beyond what we are as physical beings, our "matter," there is also a concentration, a focus, a resonance, a coherence of this energy that is our being. It is the energy that holds our matter together. Most energy healers can feel this. I can feel it. Anybody can learn to. Some people can see human auras which are made up of this coherent energy. They say this energy is not static, that it moves and flows, and through this flow, we are connected to each other, and to everything else including the Earth. They tell us everything is connected.

Now, expand that connection to the whole field of energy (because quantum physics has), to the known and unknown universe, through the three dimensions we live in, through the eleven dimensions we know about, and however many more we don't yet know for sure (current thinking says at least twenty-three), and expand it, please, at that instantaneous speed that is faster than the speed of light.

Another rather large idea.

There are traditional systems of medicine built on keeping this energy in right motion that work very well, and there are many techniques in the practice of energy medicine: Reiki is one of these. Acupuncture (which works with energy meridians in the body) is probably the best known in the West. Shiatsu is another, and there are many others.

Now, this energy relates to the experiences and emotions (stories) of our lives in a way analogous to the neuropeptides.

When we are holding on to old pain, old events that still cause us hurt or anger or grief or fear, these old events can literally show up in the energy around our bodies as places that are constricted, where energy does not flow as it should. Among people who can see this energy (they are sometimes called "color seers" in India, and the skill is thought to run in families), there are those who can literally see the constrictions. Many more people can feel energy constrictions. A medical intuitive can sense them from a distance without even looking directly at a person. I can sometimes feel them. Where the energy of our being does not flow properly is where the physical body eventually (takes a while) develops some ailment. This is a simplified explanation. Energy-healing practitioners will rightfully say that I'm not going into enough detail.

But this is enough detail to get to my point: Reframing an individual's stories of events that hurt, changing the context so that the event has use or meaning, can and does release constricted energy, just as it changes neuropeptides held in body tissue, and people's lives can and do change because of it.

There is more to think about in these changes.

Further Practice

This list barely begins to address what is available. Look on the "New Age" shelves of bookstores. Entering "Reiki" or "shiatsu," "acupuncture" or "quantum touch" or the names of any of these authors on the www will call up more information.

ABOUT KI ENERGY

Brennan, Barbara Ann. *Hands of Light: A Guide to Healing Through the Human Energy Field; a New Paradigm for the Human Being in Health, Relationships, and Disease.* New York: Pleiades Books, 1987.

_____. *Light Emerging: The Journey of Personal Healing*. New York: Bantam Books, 1993.

Brennan was a NASA meteorologist who turned energy healer. The illustrations in these books, done at her instruction, are genuinely helpful. Brennan sees more than most of us. She runs a school for energy healers.

Bruyere, Rosalyn L. *Wheels of Light: A Study of the Chakras*. Sierra Madre, CA: Bon Productions, 1989.

Rosalyn Bruyere is one of the healers who worked with Dr. Valerie V. Hunt in the research for *Infinite Mind*. She wrote her own book out of that and other experiences.

Eden, Donna with David Feinstein, Ph.D. *Energy Medicine: Balance Your Body's Energies for Optimal Health, Joy, and Vitality*. New York: Putnam, 1998.

This is a really good how-to book on using energy medicine for yourself. Eden also has instructional DVDs available.

Hunt, Ph.D., Valerie V. *Infinite Mind: Science of the Human Vibrations of Consciousness*. Malibu, CA: Malibu Publishing Co., 1996.

Hunt is a scientist, who for this book, works with a series of energy healers, measuring and documenting the effects of what they do in human beings.

Myss, Ph.D., Caroline M. *Anatomy of the Spirit: The Seven Stages of Power and Healing*. New York: Harmony Books, 1996.

_____. *Why People Don't Heal and How They Can*. New York: Harmony Books, 1997.

Myss, Ph.D., Caroline M. with C. Norman Shealy, M.D. *The Creation of Health: The Emotional, Psychological, and Spiritual Responses That Promote Health and Healing*. New York: Three Rivers Press, 1998.

A medical intuitive talks about her work. Myss was the first author I read when I was beginning to study energy medicine.

MONKEY MIND

WHEN YOU THINK about the way humans hold on to their old pain, it has all the makings of a science-fiction horror thriller.

There is in each of us a voice, a sort of commentator, that may be a product of the rational mind and our capacity for language. Now, I'm not arguing that the rational mind (or language, for that matter—heaven forbid, I'm a writer) has no value, but it is the rational mind that accepts or rejects the memes* we are given by our culture.

I'm not arguing against rational thought either. I am an enthralled lay student of human rational endeavor, particularly in quantum physics and the new cosmology. Just understand, though, this rational thought business has led to some ugly places in our history.

Maybe this internal commentator is fear-based, and a capacity of the rational mind—judgment turned difficult—contributes to it. (An example of judgment turned difficult could be someone with self-esteem problems.) Maybe the commentator is a product of the memes we accept and that same internalized hard judgment. Neurolinguistic programming calls this voice "self-talk."

No science I've read explains where the human mind's self-talk comes from, or how it developed. Julian Jaynes makes an argument, as I understand his book, for a time before humans experienced self-talk (as we know it now), perhaps as recently as three thousand years ago, in his book *The Origins of Consciousness in the Breakdown of the Bicameral Mind.* A tremendous amount of brain research is available but none I've found really addresses where self-talk comes from. NLP says self-talk can be trained in what it tells us about ourselves, and gives instruction in that endeavor. Training self-talk is a useful endeavor, but it still doesn't address the origins of the commentator.

On the other hand, every book on meditation** (ok, I haven't read all of them) includes instruction about how to learn to shut up self-talk. We are the only creatures we know of who contend with it (though how we know we're the only creatures who contend with it, I'm not sure). Some thinking says that it is a relatively recent addition to the human brain, an evolutionary experiment of which nobody yet knows the outcome. But, along with our opposing thumbs and bipedal position, it does seem to be part of what defines us as human.

Self-talk may be what Rene Descartes was talking about when he said: "I think, therefore I am." How do we think without self-talk? Descartes himself caused rather a lot of four-legged suffering in some of those moments when he wasn't lying on his Age of Reason couch because, as an extension of his rational thinking, he was convinced that animals didn't experience fear or pain because they weren't rational beings, and he cut up live ones to prove it. Howls and cries and attempts at escape were ascribed to instinct, not to fear or pain. It is a difficulty, the situations rational thinking can get you into sometimes . . .

In most people, self-talk is an ongoing critic. It is background noise if we are engaged in something that takes our attention, but it is usually more than background noise. It is a voice in the mind. Sometimes it seems to use other people's voices, sometimes our own, it uses language, and it often spends a lot of time telling us what idiots we are, how stupid we were in one situation or another. It is obsessed with its own remembrance of things past, replaying hard moments over and over again like some kind of electronic glitch, like a malfunction, in our minds. This is why "Be Here Now" (not stuck somewhere in the past or worrying about the future) is such a big idea in the world's mystical traditions. Living in the moment is a way to begin to control self-talk. Self-talk is a judge, and in most of us, it is not the least bit benevolent. It is our own personal, endlessly portable, hanging judge.

If we weren't so accustomed to it, it might come to be thought of differently. It should be thought of differently. "I am, therefore I think." Sometimes. Every once in a while. On infrequent occasions. Whenever I am able.

In all the traditions that seek enlightenment, self-talk is the first thing to address. Buddhists have several ways to think of it. One is that it is a wild elephant that you always have to feed. It is yours, but it must be trained before it will ever be of any service. Another metaphor calls it "monkey mind." Meditation is the prescribed training for the elephant or the monkey, and meditation is designed to achieve a few seconds of inner silence.

There is a traditional Buddhist teaching that says if you could truly be without those inner thoughts (self-talk) for twelve solid seconds, you would achieve enlightenment, otherwise known as union with the Divine. Twelve seconds. That number, more than anything else I know, speaks to what a hold this judge has on us.

All meditation traditions recognize that thoughts will come up during meditation, thoughts like what a fool we are for trying to do something like meditation to begin with, what a waste of time it is, etc. Monkey mind knows exactly how to get to us every time. The job of the person doing the meditation is to acknowledge those thoughts without following them and without judgment, and go back to silence. This is hard to do, much harder than it sounds. Monkey mind: "Two seconds down, only ten to go, and now you've got to start all over, you can't do it!" Thank you, monkey mind.

Carlos Castaneda*** (he mentions this in several of his books), quotes his teacher don Juan as saying this portion of our brain (the self-talk part) is a (relatively recent) "foreign installation" designed to generate hard emotions (read "energy"), which are consumed by predators we cannot see, who keep us like we keep cows, and keep us unhappy with their little installation because that is the energy they find most palatable. You don't have to believe the statement literally to find it a compelling metaphor.

Monkey mind can be trained: traditionally, mantras and meditation are useful; these days, affirmations are the fashion. NLP's retraining of self-talk uses affirmations, but the intent of NLP is to turn self-talk into an ally instead of an enemy, not to silence it. The Toltec tradition (I'm speaking of the energy tradition, not the Toltec civilization) teaches other ways of achieving that inner silence (and much more), but the parallels are all there. They are all talking about shutting up a destructive monkey mind. With discipline, monkey mind can be made to let go a little. The cultivating of inner silence is a way to collect more personal energy, but monkey mind, because it is a condition of being human, cannot be made to go away entirely—except, maybe, by the very most disciplined of us, Buddha for instance.

Now, to get to the relationship of monkey mind to the stories of our lives, we have to think again of the neuropeptides in our bodies, and of the energy that makes up our being. Every time monkey mind goes back over an unpleasant event in our experience (and given monkey mind and hard experience, it is usually again and again and again), we get a fresh wash of the very same neuropeptides we got in the original event. Chemically in our body and electrically in our brains, experience and memory of experience do the very same thing. The body does not distinguish between them. And this does not change until we find some new way to think of a specific experience.

The same is true of energy: going back over hard experience in monkey mind reinforces energy constrictions in the same way it provides fresh neuropeptides, because, again, experience and memory of experience do the same thing in the body.

So, when I add a passage by a dragon or successfully reframe a story, I am changing the way monkey mind has to think of a specific event, so monkey mind doesn't just get to pour more and more of the same neuropeptides into the body or continually

constrict the energy or, to use don Juan's vision, feed our large
and hungry predators their preferred food.

＊ THE ASTERISKS ＊

*Memes: The subject of memes is a study unto itself (as is so
much in this book, the big risk of omnivorous reading) and I'm
touching lightly on a much larger body of work. I'm touching on
it because so much of what makes the society we live in is based
in memes. We live in meme houses, we drive meme cars, we dress
in meme clothes, we think about our own stories out of the
memes we are given, we judge others by the memes we hold.
Memes are the very box we want (and need) to be able to think
outside of occasionally, so knowing a little about what they are is
genuinely useful.

A meme is a unit of cultural information that we get verbally
or by repeated action. Richard Brodie (in *Virus of the Mind*)
described memes as a society's DNA. J. M. Balkin (in *Cultural
Software*) described them as society's software. A definition from
the online encyclopedia Wikipedia reads: "A contagious idea that
replicates itself like a virus because it is passed from mind to
mind. Memes can represent ideas, parts of ideas, language, tunes,
designs, skills, moral or aesthetic values," and that is not the
entirety of the list. *Random House Webster's Dictionary* (second edition) is a little lower key: "A cultural item that is transmitted by
repetition in a manner analogous to the biological transmission
of genes."

Advertising functions by using memes to create demand for
a specific product. The alphabet song you learned in kindergarten
installed a very useful set of memes. "Seatbelts Save Lives" is a useful meme. The evolution of the usage of the word "*bad*" is an ongoing meme. "Wash your hands before you eat." "Wear clean under-
wear in case you are hit by a car and have to go to the hospital."

Memes are not inherently harmful, and nobody is suggesting
they are. The problem with them is that we pick them up without
realizing we've gotten them. And if we are not aware of having

gotten them, the danger is that we won't ever question their validity. And every one of us lives with an astonishing assortment of memes as if they were true.

A few of the all time loser memes: The world is flat. Christianity is the only true religion and heretics should be burned at the stake. Those who are different from me are lesser. Women are the property of their husbands. Spare the rod and spoil the child.

Needless to say, this is not the entirety of a list of loser memes. Identifying loser memes would be an interesting way to study cultural history.

My all-time favorite on the meme list arrived in my consciousness in the late 1960s: "Question authority." It says I should not only question anything that sets itself up as authority, but I should also question my own questioning lest it become another authority. This is a personal Zen koan, like the sound of one hand clapping, an idea that keeps the mind wrapping around and around itself as a kind of meditation.

◄ ►

**Meditation. You can read every meditation book written and you will know a lot about it but you will not know what it is until you do it. Meditation is a body-learning experience, it is not something that happens in the rational mind. And like most body-learning experiences, it takes some practice.

My own practice breaks a lot of rules. It is my favorite meme in operation. First, I usually don't sit, I lie down. I can do a sitting meditation and a walking meditation, but I prefer to lie down. I orient myself north-south, but it doesn't seem to matter which direction my head is. It does seem to matter a little that I'm aligned with Earth's magnetic field. I lie flat on my back, no pillow. Sometimes I shut my eyes, it is the easier practice, but you must keep from going to sleep. A theta state is a light sleep, a dreaming sleep; a delta state is deep sleep. Delta is easy to fall into with your eyes closed. The harder practice (but far more useful in the long run, it is the first step in learning to see energy) is to keep the eyes open and learn to not focus the vision, to use soft focus and see with peripheral vision. This, too, takes practice. Looking slightly up instead of straight ahead helps, crossing the eyes just slightly also helps. Next, I clinch my muscles in groups and relax, clinch and relax. I breathe several intentional breaths from the diaphragm, as deep as I can, and after I've done a few, my breathing comes from the diaphragm without my having to think about it. (Diaphragmatic breathing is the big advantage of lying down. It is hard not to breathe with your diaphragm when you are lying down.) And then, I try to shut up monkey mind. If all else fails— I have a few years of practice at this, and all else can still fail—I make a quiet noise that is easy to make ("ah" or "om," those two syllables mean specific things from the Sanskrit; my understanding is that "ah" invites the Divine, "om" gives thanks to the Divine). I make these sounds at the lowest register I can comfortably do with each exhale. I want to feel my sound in my body as much as hear it. I make the exhales long and slow, and focus on making the sound smooth. I try to let things in my mind leave with the exhales. I try to open up my throat and chest and let the sound deepen as it happens, and as I relax, it does that. I am going from a beta state to an alpha state in my brain. I imagine the sound to be the same sort of sound a cat makes when it is purring, and I want the pleasure and joy and grace of purring throughout my body.

Then, the trick: I quit the sound and keep the feeling. Things change when I quit the sound. What was sound becomes an energy that feels like joy running through me. I can feel it. I can direct it. I run it like a rollercoaster through my body if that's my inclination, run it till I almost get the giggles. Thoughts come up, of course, sometimes images. My job is to acknowledge them without judging or following them, let the thought go and find the feeling again. I go from alpha to theta in my brain. My goal in this state is to be made entirely of love and joy and give it away to all life. What a cool job it is. I stay in that state for an hour or so. I usually do my practice at night because it doesn't matter how long I stay with it if I start when I'm ready for bed and I am almost never interrupted at night. I love being in that state. The longer I stay, the less sleep I need. The usual rule of thumb is that an hour of deep meditation equals about three hours of sleep, so if I spend the entire night that way, it doesn't matter. I've never spent an entire night: an hour or so is usually about all I can do at a time.

At first, I was inclined to just fall asleep, but that doesn't happen much now, my body has learned the difference between the meditative state and the sleep state. Many people struggle with that problem at first.

I have outlined my personal variation of the loving-kindness meditation and how I get there. There are lots of other intents for meditation: problem-solving and healing are a couple of them. I do loving-kindness because that is what I need, and consistent practice at a specific meditation helps. There are also lots of other ways to do meditation: sitting, walking (keep the eyes soft-focused, use peripheral vision), ecstatic dancing (a Sufi tradition); day-to-day jobs, like cleaning house or mowing the lawn, can also be done with monkey mind shut off or at least turned way down. There are good specific how-to instructions easily available, but bottom line is that the time spent out of monkey mind is of huge service to the body and the being. Holding the alpha and/or theta state and consciousness at the same time (a description of what we usually think of as meditation) is a powerful place and worth every minute of the time invested to learn how to get there.

There is more, and this comes with *a holy lot* of practice. It is possible to go from the alpha state (lower hertz than normal waking consciousness) to gamma (a state of higher hertz in the brain than beta, which is normal waking consciousness). This is truly heightened awareness. Both sides of the brain are engaged equally and the mind is *focused* by holding an intention to the exclusion of everything else. (In my practice, described above, that intention is to *be* love and joy.) This is not, for me or for most who do meditation, an everyday event. I've achieved this state maybe four or five times in the course of some years of meditation practice. But this state can be, it has been, measured by analyzing the hertz levels in the brain during meditation. People who do a lot of meditation can achieve it with some consistency. (Some of the Dalai Lama's brother monks were found to be astonishingly consistent in attaining the gamma state.) This is a long-term goal and you will know it if you get there.

⊣ ⊢

***Carlos Castaneda and his writing. I understand how easy it is to dismiss Castaneda's work. Not science, not anthropology, not validated in any traditional way (he perpetually "lost" his field notes), from an author who made a life-long habit of lying like a rug, and the first two books of the series have a whole lot to do with ingesting hallucinogenic drugs. (FYI: the rest of the books do not encourage drug use.) An industry has been made out of Castaneda's heritage (Cleargreen and others) and I know how suspect that is. So I do know the reasons to doubt.

I've also read about how ugly and damaging to other people the guru phase of Castaneda's life became.

So let me speak about why I am still interested in the work.

Castaneda claims to have documented, over a series of several years and best-selling books, the teachings of a Toltec (energy tradition) nagual he called don Juan. The books recount astonishing experience. Don Juan's intention was the opening of perception and the efficient use of personal energy. Buddhism's intention is enlightenment and if you read texts of Buddhist practice, there are real parallels to what don Juan taught. So don Juan was teaching a version of the search for enlightenment, just not by those words.

Don Juan's first instruction to Castaneda was about shutting up monkey mind, followed closely by learning to give up the ego. Don Juan taught letting go of the past (he had several techniques). He taught some very specific meditations—one was a walking meditation that included a way to keep the mind focused by concentrating on holding the hands in a certain position. He also taught more traditional kinds of meditation. His "not-doings," looking for and focusing on spaces not things, and using peripheral vision are all great and time-honored meditation techniques. Don Juan taught several traditional siddhis, like seeing energy or knowing events in advance. Buddhist teaching says the siddhis are distractions from the true spiritual search, and advises never to focus on them. Don Juan spoke about the ancient "sorcerers" of his tradition getting caught in them by thinking they had more power than they did and dying from it. Don Juan kept the three essentials of Buddhist teaching: a relationship with an "enlightened" teacher, a regular practice, and a connection to a supportive community. There are more comparisons, including some aspects of don Juan and his group's departure from this world, as recounted in Castaneda's work, by skipping the usual dying process. There are similar stories of yogis choosing a time to leave life and doing it. So, if you read the Castaneda books with Buddhist teaching in mind, the backbone of them is a description of a path.

Some claim that Castaneda is straight fiction, but this idea gets shaken a little because there is some truth in the specifics. Don Juan's "seeing" is an example. Don Juan says people seen as energy are luminous egg-shaped creatures with a place on that egg where perception is assembled, and he calls that the assemblage point. Now, have I ever seen people as egg-shaped creatures? No. Have I ever seen the point where perception is assembled? No. Well, what have I seen? I have seen what is traditionally known as auras. I cannot see them consistently, but a few times, I have seen the energy around a human body. Being stuck at a lecture in the middle of a row of seats with a boring speaker in front of a solid background helps this endeavor considerably. Don Juan says you have to shift your assemblage point to change your perception sufficiently to see this energy. I have to shift hertz levels in my brain, go from normal beta to alpha (like meditation) before it can happen to me, and I have to use soft-focused vision. I can't do that without the time and concentration it takes for me to achieve a meditative state, hence the value of the boring speaker.

The most magical of my "seeings" happened late at night when I was doing meditation. My dog started to bark at something. I wanted to stay in the meditation in spite of the noise, but the dog was truly persistent, so I rolled over to look out my bedroom window into the front yard. My bedroom is upstairs so I was looking down. The outside glowed with a cool, flowing light I had never seen before. I could see the shape of the magnolia tree as light; I could see a glow flowing across the grass, and then I noticed a brighter elongated flowing silver shape that moved close to the ground, and I watched it. My perception changed over the next minute or so, and the shape became a possum that was almost invisible in the dark. What did I see? I think I saw energy, but maybe I've just read too much Castaneda.

Another of the practices that don Juan (via Castaneda) taught is "lucid dreaming." This is another practice for controlling the mind. It is also a Buddhist practice. It is also hard to learn to do with any sort of consistency because it takes a quality Buddhists call "diamond mind," which is being in the moment and observing the moment at the same time (hard enough) and then, keeping that state beyond the threshold of sleep. But it is another endeavor for which don Juan gave specific how-to instructions if you can wade through enough Castaneda to get to them. And they are how-to instructions that work. The first step in lucid dreaming is to carry a conscious intention across the threshold of sleep. Don Juan's first instruction is to work at it until you can remember to look at your hands when you are asleep, as good a conscious intention as any to carry across that threshold.

If Castaneda is writing the experience he claims as truth, and he does claim that in print, he had a most extraordinary opportunity, and he spent most of it navel gazing, or in denial, or in paroxysms of egomania with little understanding of what an opening of perception might mean. He spent so very much time just not getting it at all that reading the books he wrote is a real frustration. You have to shovel Castaneda out of the way to get to the teaching.

If he is writing fiction as some claim, he is a truly compelling storyteller and he did research somewhere, because don Juan's instruction is too close to a recognized, traditional perception-opening path to be concocted entirely out of the blue. The map of a path has value, but if the work is pure fiction, the fundamental lie—that he recounts his own experience—creates a credibility problem.

On the other hand—I do go back and forth—much of his book *The Fire from Within* reads like a (poetic) description of what quantum physics now tells us is actually true of this world. So did Carlos Castaneda study quantum physics when he wasn't off in Mexico jumping into an abyss?

I suspect the truth is that somewhere, somehow, in the course of anthropological research (he did do that), there was a "resource" who came to be called don Juan, and that Castaneda did set out on a path and in the course of recounting experience, he became a fabulist who filled a *huge* need in his time.

It would be really hard not to be a fabulist over the course of so many books and so much time, and it would be terribly hard for Castaneda to ignore the demand for more that came after he published the first of those books.

On the most basic level of human endeavor, it is impossible not to try to give meaning to experience; equally impossible not to want and seek the experience of mystery. And memory itself has never been a particularly dependable reporter of facts. Somewhere in all that lies a very long, very slippery slope.

We are, by the way our brains are structured, storytellers, god seekers, and myth makers. This is the ultimate of slippery slopes. Plato, if you remember, banned poets from his republic. They are dangerous because they put this stuff into language and seek audiences to listen to it, and people like to listen.

We each choose the details (and make the myths) out of the stories we tell, and then set out to live those myths. This is fascinating stuff energy-wise, and (oh, paradox!) part of my interest in don Juan is that he is so determined to bust that meme-minding, myth-keeping in his student. It is the way to open perception and *see*. He didn't succeed. In Castaneda's telling, those books are ultimately a recounting of a mostly failed effort on the part of the teacher, and part of the reason for the failure is that Castaneda couldn't ever change, in any basic way, how he thought about himself.

In the meantime, I can no more prove that don Juan was real than I can prove that Buddha was real. For that matter, I cannot prove Jesus Christ of the stories I got as a child in the Baptist church was real either, but all of them are teachers and the nature of this world is such that you best take your teachers where you can find them. In the business of opening perception, I find don Juan, who or whatever he was, as recounted by the tremendously suspect (Trickster?) Castaneda, to be a teacher of mine. And if the instructions work, from Christ or Buddha or don Juan or the Dalai Lama or a shaman friend or an energy healer or a community of like-minded people, then you should make use of them.

Further Practice

ABOUT THE EVOLUTION OF THE HUMAN BRAIN

Jaynes, Julian. *The Origins of Consciousness in the Breakdown of the Bicameral Mind.* New York: Houghton Mifflin, 2000.

This is radical thinking and not widely accepted at the time it was published. But, then, Darwin wasn't accepted when he published either.

ABOUT MEDITATION

There is a tremendous amount available on meditation, but reading alone simply will not get you to the practice of it. A teacher is tremendously useful to begin a practice. Sounds True publishing company (soundstrue.com) offers audio from some of the better teachers available today, including how-to instructions for meditation. Put on a CD, use the earphones, and learn this stuff.

His Holiness the Dalai Lama, translated by Jeffery Hopkins, Ph.D. *How to Practice: The Way to a Meaningful Life.* New York: Pocket Books, 2002.

This book is alarmingly simple, he teaches a loving-kindness practice, he's writing for Westerners, and in this world, he is the horse's mouth.

Kornfield, Jack. *After the Ecstasy, the Laundry: How the Heart Grows Wise on the Spiritual Path.* New York, Bantam Books, 2000.

This is Jack Kornfield's recounting of his practice; I like his style of writing.

McTaggart, Lynne. *The Field: The Quest for the Secret Force of the Universe.* New York: HarperCollins, 2002.

_____. *The Intention Experiment: Using Your Thoughts to Change Your Life and the World.* New York: Free Press, 2007.

In *The Field*, McTaggart chases down the science. In *The Intention Experiment*, she includes meditation instructions as a way to use the field. You will find, in these very readable books, the specific numbers for the energy that flows through the hands of energy healers, MRI readings of brain activity during meditation, etc., and be able to understand scientists' current thinking about what all this means. Read the book and participate in her intention experiments.

If you read no other books from the Further Practice sections, read these two by Lynne McTaggart. It is helpful to read *The Field* first.

Thurman, Robert and Tad Wise. *Circling the Sacred Mountain: A Spiritual Adventure Through the Himalayas.* New York: Bantam Books, 1999.

This is an account of a particular practice. Wise is the doubter. The parts of this book I love are Thurman's lessons; I'm not big on Wise's angst. Thurman has written a lot for Westerners on the subject of Buddhism; he's a good teacher.

ABOUT MEMES

Balkin, J. M. *Cultural Software: A Theory of Ideology.* New Haven, CT: Yale University Press, 1998.

This book is a recommended source of information about memes.

Brodie, Richard. *Virus of the Mind: The New Science of the Meme.* Seattle: Integral Press, 1996.

This is the red-flag warning book; you'll feel like you need to wash your brain. With bleach.

Hubbard, Barbara Marx. *Conscious Evolution: Awakening Our Social Potential.* Navato, CA: New World Library, 1998.

This book has a good chapter on memes.

ABOUT HOW STORIES WORK IN OUR LIVES

McAdams, Dan P. *The Stories We Live By: Personal Myths and the Making of the Self.* New York: William Morrow & Company, 1993.

McAdams has several books worth reading about how stories work in our lives. His is a rather academic approach, but readable, and I like to check in with the academy occasionally. McAdams (on this subject) is one of the writers I go back for more of.

ABOUT THE TOLTEC (ENERGY) TRADITION

Abelar, Taisha. *The Sorcerer's Crossing: A Woman's Journey.* New York: Viking Arkana, 1992.

As with Florinda Donner, Abelar says she was from the same group of don Juan's trainees as Castaneda, so she was also a student of don Juan and his colleagues. Her (and Donner's) recounted experience is vastly different from Castaneda's.

Castaneda, Carlos.

The Teachings of don Juan: A Yaqui Way of Knowledge. New York: Simon & Schuster, 1973. (First published by the University of California Press in 1968.)

A Separate Reality. New York: Simon & Schuster, 1971.

Journey to Ixtlan. New York: Simon & Schuster, 1972.

Tales of Power. New York: Simon & Schuster, 1974.

The Second Ring of Power. New York: Simon & Schuster, 1979.

The Eagle's Gift. New York: Simon & Schuster, 1981.

The Fire from Within. New York: Simon & Schuster, 1984.

The Power of Silence. New York: Simon & Schuster, 1987.

The Art of Dreaming. New York: HarperCollins, 1993.

The Active Side of Infinity. New York: HarperCollins, 1998.

This is the series of books that recount Castaneda's endeavors with his teacher, don Juan; Castaneda doesn't begin to understand much of what is going on in the extraordinary experience until *The Eagle's Gift*, but you won't understand at all if you just start there. I suggest you read the books in chronological order. Much of the material essentially recounts the same experience over and over, it is just that Castaneda knows (or reveals) more with each telling.

Donner, Florinda. *Being-in-Dreaming: An Initiation into the Sorcerors' World*. San Francisco: HarperSanFrancisco, 1991.

_____. *The Witch's Dream: A Healer's Way of Knowledge*. New York: Simon & Schuster, 1985.

As with Abelar, Donner says she was from the same group of don Juan's trainees as Castaneda, so she was also a student of don Juan and his colleagues. Her (and Abelar's) recounted experience is vastly different from Castaneda's.

Nelson, Mary Carroll. *Beyond Fear—A Toltec Guide to Freedom and Joy: The Teachings of don Miguel Ruiz*. Tulsa, OK: Council Oak Books, 1997.

This is a philosophy text that sets up a useful way to think. In the previous chapter, I listed Ruiz's *Four Agreements*. They are Ruiz's basic practice.

Sanchez, Victor. *The Toltec Path of Recapitulation: Healing Your Past to Free Your Soul*. Rochester, VT: Bear & Company, 2001.

This is one of several Sanchez books available. Sanchez and company say they are carrying on Castaneda's teaching. There are others out there who claim the same thing. This is a practice book that will make more sense if you've read Castaneda, but you can read it without Castaneda. Again, just reading the book is not practicing recapitulation, like reading about meditation is not the practice. Recapitulation is a way to collect personal energy from past events in your life. Seems to work (yes it does). It is similar to the shamanic idea of soul retrieval, just the do-it-yourself variation.

Wallace, Amy. *Sorcerer's Apprentice: My Life with Carlos Castaneda.* Berkeley, CA: Frog Books, 2003.

This is a cult-busting book—Castaneda and his cohorts are less than wonderful human beings in this recounting of Wallace's experience with them. She was Castaneda's main squeeze for a while.

The Work of Imagination in the Body and in the Energy Around the Body

To understand how imagination works in the energy of the body, let me describe what experiencing an emotion does to this energy.

I asked a dowser for this demonstration and I was invited to his home to see it—I drove sixty-plus miles to get there. I was still living with the remnants of the spider wound when I did this. Brown recluse bites can take a long time to heal; there are stories of bites not healing for a year or more. The Reiki I was getting helped the healing: I was actually progressing rather quickly, and I was trying to learn about this energy the Reiki people were able to channel. The visit to the dowser was recommended by one of my teachers.

Nobody can explain how or why dowsing works unless you talk about energy, and even then, it is hard to address. There is a another kind of dowsing besides the two discussed here, using a pendulum, that users say offers an access to the subconscious (or to the zero point field—there is some thinking that suggests that the individual subconscious is our personal access to the zero point field). And there is endless variation beyond this, like using a pendulum and a map to find water, a pendulum and a chart of the body for illness, a pendulum and a grid for yes and no answers . . . More, the art of dowsing does not seem to work equally for everyone who tries to do it. I'm told it can be learned (there are certainly plenty of how-to books; there are also dowsers' conventions and dowsing workshops available), but when I went to see this demonstration, dowsing did not work very well for me (it still doesn't) or for the teacher who sent me on this expedition. I'll say this though: holding good dowsing rods in your hands can be a very odd experience. Something moves them, and it doesn't feel like it is you doing it . . .

So I went on this sixty-mile trip to visit the dowser with a certain skepticism, but an interest too.

What I did know about dowsing (read: "what I had seen with my own eyes") is that some people are able to find underground water by dowsing, and twenty years before I had seen a water dowser's forked stick turn decisively toward the ground in the corner of a field, and that was the place he said to dig a well. The stick had turned toward the ground less decisively in other places. The process took a couple of hours to complete. This dowser was an old man. He didn't want me to take pictures of him working. Friends had hired him; they'd bought a piece of land that backed up on national forest, they eventually built a house on the property, but finding water was a first priority. I was invited by them to watch this man, and he wasn't much pleased by having an audience, never mind the pictures. But he did the job. My friends dug their well where he said to; they found good water and lots of it.

But this is East Tennessee and underground water is not rare. We live on limestone that is riddled with water passages.

But the dowser found a really good flow of water not very deep (about sixty feet) in the ground. In the business of digging wells, the deeper they are, the more expensive it is to dig them. (Digging a well is actually boring a hole in the ground till you get to the source of water). Sixty feet down is a cheap well. Wells that are three or four hundred feet deep are not uncommon.

I was ambivalent then about what I had seen. I questioned it because the memes I lived with said it was not possible.

This second time with a dowser, twenty years later, I *knew* there was such a thing as an energy that could make a tremendous amount of difference in the pain of the spider wound, and I had been listening to my shaman friend and other energy healers about how this energy worked. And this dowser is, among other things, a medical dowser. He uses his dowsing rods to find places on people's bodies where energy is constricted. The first thing he did when I stepped into his house—he met me at the front door with his dowsing rods in hand—was ask me to remove my shoes and put on a pair of guest slippers; the second was a gesture to be silent, and then he ran his metal dowsing rods (he wasn't using a forked stick) over my body, front and back, maybe eight or ten inches away from me. The rods were spinning until they stopped and came to a point. Now, this man ran his dowsing rods over *everything.* When the dowsing rods stopped, they were pointing to the place on my back/butt. "What's there?" Finding the bite was a test I hadn't requested, but he did it because that's what he does. With everybody. Didn't take him a whole minute to find it. He didn't know beforehand about the spider bite and he couldn't see it, I had on all my clothes. But he—like the Reiki folks and the shaman—found it, he said, by the disruption in the energy around the wound. The dowsing rods pointed to it.

He said he was able to work the rods—or have the rods work for him—because he was able to get his own expectations out of the way enough to do it. That's why he didn't want me to say anything at first. "It's harder to look for something I think I'm going to find, too much of me in it then."

I had been instructed to ask him to show me what emotion does to the energy body. The value of the dowsing rods is that they make the answers visible. I could see what the dowsing rods did and when. We'd moved to his living room by then.

"Ok," he said, "be neutral."

It was an odd order but I set out to comply; I thought about the drive I'd just done to meet him. He backed away, giving me a little time to get into whatever emotional state was neutral; then he began walking toward me, the dowsing rods—one in each hand—pointed in front of him. They weren't spinning this time, they were relatively still. At about eight feet away from me, the dowsing rods crossed and stayed there.

"That's the edge of your normal energy body," he said. "Now, think of something that makes you angry."

I thought of a specific incident from the time of the pitching practice that had made me genuinely furious. Again, a little time—seconds—for me to get into the feeling and he walked toward me again, and at about a foot and a half away from me, the dowsing rods crossed in front of him again.

"See that? Anger eats you alive," he said. I thought of don Juan's predators who preferred the harder emotions as food, and found, in that moment, the traditional idiom the dowser had used rather discomforting.

"Ok," he said, "think of something you love."

I thought of a favorite four-legged, the dog who lives with me. The dowser walked away from me again, through a door and into another room, forty feet or so distant, then he began walking slowly toward me. At about twenty-four feet away, the dowsing rods in his hands crossed for a third time.

"Loving anything sends energy through you like you've turned on a river," he said.

I asked if he had expectations for that experiment and, and if he did, wouldn't that affect it?

"I do know the energy is going to be there, but I don't know where it is going to be. It varies. You'd be surprised."

And then he did the whole thing again, with a catch, to show me it hadn't been accidental the first time. I was to feel something but keep the emotion to myself—I went through love, neutral and anger again, not particularly imaginative except I tried to think of different things to be angry about and love—and he named what the emotion was by the distance at which the dowsing rods crossed. The results varied by a foot or two with the exception of that "edge of anger." It was, he explained, my feeling that determined when the dowsing rods crossed, things I could imagine that brought up feeling in me. Nothing else was happening to me except what I was doing in my own head.

To return to my point from the dowsing digression, emotion (in this example, neutrality, anger and love), what we feel, what we feel as we say something, think something, what we really feel about anything makes a big difference in our energy. The dowsing rods just make it visible.

Now, we already know that the individual's imagination can be a powerful healer. We know, for instance, that it is helpful to instruct cancer patients to imagine their white blood cells as soldiers doing battle with an intruder, or (for those not inclined to war images) as a corps of determined house cleaners removing the cells that aren't needed in the body.* This is a very personal kind of storytelling. We know this imagining works better if people have a sense of where in their body they are sending the white blood cells (and their assorted assistants), literally what the territory looks like, where it is and how to get there. We know this imagining is best accomplished in a meditative state with monkey mind shut down as much as possible during the time of the imagining. And we know repetition of the exercise seems to help healing for a couple of reasons: practice in shutting off monkey mind makes us better at doing it, and we literally put a fresh corps of those house cleaners into our bloodstream when we successfully imagine it.

We also know that this imagining works like gangbusters for some people, but minimally or not at all for others. We also know athletes use a similar sort of imagining, running races or playing games in their heads before the real event, and, for some, it seems to make a significant difference in their performance.

The suggested uses of this kind of imaginative work increase daily. Many of them are pretty shallow without the application of some elbow grease; for instance: "Imagine Yourself Successful!" But there is no question that deep imagining can make a tremendous difference in health and in athletic performance, and imagining yourself successful with the application of some elbow grease is a real way to accomplish at least some of that success.

The difference between people for whom imagining works and those for whom it does not is the difference between those who have an emotional, feeling experience with the exercise and those who have an intellectual, rational experience. For imagining to work, you have to feel what you are imagining. It is the feeling (emotion) that has energy. Feeling something deeply, even something new, works like experience (or the memory of experience) in the mind and the chemistry of the body. A rational intellectual experience does not do the same thing in the body.**

One lesson in all this is a medical one: send out those house cleaners with love for your body and your life, and not with anger at whatever needs cleaning up. Avoid the anger. It gives you far less energy to work with. Remember the idiom: anger eats you alive.

The application to the story work is this: for both the teller and the listener, a story lives in the mind differently than a novel or a movie or even a traditional play, because a story asks for deeper imagining, it asks you to create the sensory experience around what you are hearing. In films, the sensory experience is provided. It is a key part of the filmmaker's art. Watching a film can be an alpha-trance state: it usually is. In a novel, you are given descriptions in words, but you still get the descriptions: weather, terrain, architecture, decor, along with the physiognomy of characters. You also get thoughts and emotions of the characters. A novel asks for more imagining than a movie but the details are still provided. With a play, sensory experience is supplied with costumes, sets, lights and actors. A play may ask more of you than a movie, but the sensory experience is still more of a given compared to listening to a storyteller. Hearing a story uses a different process in the brain.

I use literal storytelling a lot in my community work because an untrained actor can handle narrative better than they can handle a scene in which they need to "become" a character. Even in the context of a character telling a story (like Pen Bascome's murder sermon, or the Burn story in which the woman tells of her stepmother trying to burn her when she was a child), I use a story format, not a traditional scene.*** When I put a story onstage, a deeper imagining on the part of the storyteller and from the audience is obliged because of how a story works in the human mind. And we know imagining makes a measurable difference in a person's energy by the way the body responds to a real or imagined event.****

⇥ THE ASTERISKS ⇤

*There is more to say about imagining for health, and how it works, and I am being inaccurate (not to mention negligent) if I don't address it. There is always energy—a lack of it, constriction—with "dis-ease," and for imagining to work, the causes of the problem need to be addressed or the constriction in the energy won't go away. Humans get sick for reasons. The variety of reasons is endless but, short of direct environmental problems, there is almost always some emotional cause. Illness can be caused by a specific event, but it is more likely caused by a long-held attitude or an ongoing situation—the etiology of dis-ease is not the least bit simple. And—worse news—it won't be fixed by anyone but the person who has the problem. There is considerable understanding of this in the medical field (just ask your doctor), the field just doesn't use terms as specific as "cause" and there is no verification by scientific study. The discussions I have read are mostly in "medical experience" literature and they are often observations about who survives cancer and who does not.

Energy healers, on the other hand, are very willing to name the relationship of feeling or attitude to dis-ease. It is basic to the energy-healing endeavor, but it is never easy news to hear because it gives the person who is sick real responsibility for their condition. Most of us have some trouble accepting that responsibility.

Let me use myself (again) as illustration: I've had a hyperthyroid problem; it has been some years since the medical diagnosis of my situation (the diagnosis came during my pitching practice; that pitching business was an uncomfortable education), but I've had an inclination toward the problem longer than that.

According to Louise Hay, in her book *Heal Your Body A–Z*, hyperthyroid trouble is a physical expression of "rage at being left out." My shaman friend (the man who told me the spider bite was big medicine) said something very similar. He named the rage. He named it by what he could feel in the energy around my body. I find Louise Hay's odd little book downright scary: that naming fits me far better than I like. So I have to own those emotions, admit them, deal with them, and begin to *let them go* in order to address the problems that anger makes in my body. (Now you know why a loving-kindness meditation is my choice of practice.) Making use of the information about anger and the meditation and the imagining I did (and still do) has let me hold on to my thyroid despite allopathic medicine's recommendation, and my body's thyroid production is normal. Can I still get enraged? I'm really good at it. I can tell myself versions of events that generate anger in me whether the actual events warrant that thinking or not. It is a pattern I have set over the course of my life. The physical symptoms of hyperthyroidism (elevated heartbeat, disrupted bowels, inability to sleep, heat intolerance, lack of energy, and an assortment of other inconveniences) come on fast if I don't deal with those feelings. Does all this mean I can never get angry without getting sick? No, it doesn't. Some events warrant anger. I just don't get to hold on to the anger. Holding on to anger, nursing anger, is what brings on symptoms in my body.

This letting go of anger (essentially, I am breaking a habit of my being) is the hardest thing I've ever tried to learn to do.

This situation is true, say the energy-healing traditions, for anything that goes wrong with the body, short of direct environmental causes. So, for imagining to be of service for the healing of the body, there has to be some understanding of the cause of the problem (and the realigning of that energy); then the life-affirming imagining directed at the problem really can do wonders toward the restoration of health and good order.

⊰ ⊱

**Another look at imagining: my brother, the neurolinguistic programmer, says that to imagine something in the first person is called "associative imagining." That's when you get emotion with the imagining. For instance, when I think of riding my horse, I can think of myself as if I were in motion on her back, looking at the world over her ears, and that is associative, first-person imagining. I get a rush of the feeling (joy, excitement) of being on her back by just thinking about it that way. I can also think of myself as standing off to the side watching me ride the same horse. That's "disassociative imagining." I can observe my performance as a rider from this position, and that can be very useful, but I do not get the feelings of joy and excitement from it.

Disassociative imagining has tremendous use because it lessens the intensity of an experience. "So," says the psychologist to his patient, "you are very angry. How does being so angry make you feel?" The question disassociates the patient from his original anger. Fine, says NLP (and psychology), you can get the anger or fear or whatever in control by disassociative thinking, but you eventually have to deal with the anger or fear through associative imagining or (worse case) you'll make a sociopath out of the patient, someone who is so disconnected from his own real emotion that he has little feeling and no empathy at all.

So NPL tells you that for imagining to work as a healing endeavor, it has to be associative, first-person imagining. This is not different from what I've said about the value of feeling. It is just another way to talk about it, and an understanding of two very different ways to use imagining. So, for healing, I ride (I do like riding things) a white blood cell to the site in my body that needs to be cleaned, or in the case of the hyperthyroid, I imagine a control knob on my thyroid and I journey into my body and turn it down a little (associative imagining), instead of watching or directing the event from the side (disassociative imagining). I imagine myself literally helping with the work to be done.

⊰ ⊱

***Traditional thinking about writing for the theater says I did both those scenes (the Pen Bascome murder story and the Burn story) wrong. In the Pen Bascome story, I should have showed onstage the confrontation between Pen Bascome and his killer, and not just told about it. To do that, I would have had to make a whole play about that single story. We would have needed to see the two men as children; we would have needed to see the killing of Bascome; we would have needed to see the white man come in to the newspaper to tell the story he wanted printed. We'd need to see him hire a black man sometime later. And then, finally, we could see the confrontation at the Pearly Gates. It could be a good play, and in other situations I might have chosen to write the story that way, but the elaboration would not have accomplished what was wanted for the community I was working with at the time. Same is true with the Burn story. We would have witnessed the ax business, the chase, and the burning long before we got to see the woman cooking supper.

One advantage of using storytelling is that I can move through time and space much more efficiently than any other way: think quantum literature, think of storytelling as using available cosmic wormholes. Second, with storytelling, I do not have to ask a community performer who cannot handle the job very well to play the sheriff or the burned child or the abusive stepmother. And if I tell the story well, I can actually get a more powerful and longer-lasting impact with storytelling because the listener has to do some associative imagining, thereby participating in the process of making the story in his own head. These are useful dynamics to think about in making work that has real resonance in a place.

⊣ ⊢

****Masks: According to Paul Ekman, Ph.D., his teacher Silvan Tompkins, and his research collaborator Wallace Friesen, it is impossible to hide real feeling, no matter how we come by that feeling, and no matter what it is. Our faces give it away. It is involuntary. Changes can be tiny and hard to catch if someone it trying to hide something, but the changes are still readable to someone who knows what to look for. Police, airport guards and others are being taught these face-reading skills these days, but the idea is older and bigger.

There is a practice for teaching empathy in shamanic tradition in which the shaman's students study a series of masks. The masks are designed specifically for the study and the students' job is to contort their faces to match a mask as closely as possible. The skill to be acquired is in really matching the masks, and then, to learn to find in their bodies what the contortion of their own faces make them feel.

This is an eye-opening exercise (literally, you are surprised by it and your eyes open wider), because putting your face in a specific gesture *makes* feeling in your body just like having a feeling in your body *makes* a specific response to it on your face. It works both ways. Paul Ekman and Wallace Friesen noticed this, too, as they spent time sitting across a table from one another making faces, trying to figure out which set of muscles went with which emotion.

It doesn't take special masks to do this. All you need is to be observant any time there are people around to watch, and some time to practice making their face with your own. You'll find, when you start fitting your face to others, the feeling that goes with that face will arrive in the area of your solar plexus.

Your mama used to tell you if you made a face too much, you'd get it stuck like that . . .

Further Practice

ABOUT DOWSING

You will find a wealth of dowsing material if you Google "dowsing" on the www: water dowsing, treasure dowsing. Almost anything you can ask a question about can be dowsed in some fashion. The results are often surprising, but you are on your own to determine their validity.

Grace, Raymon. *The Future Is Yours: Do Something About It!* Self-published: RaymonGrace.com.

I've seen this man speak and seen him work. The book can be purchased from Grace's website: RaymonGrace.com.

Webster, Richard. *Dowsing for Beginners: The Art of Discovering Water, Treasure, Gold, Oil, and Artifacts.* St. Paul, MN: Llewellyn Publications, 1996.

A how-to book about dowsing.

ABOUT EMOTIONAL CAUSES OF HEALTH PROBLEMS

Hay, Louise L. *Heal Your Body A–Z: The Mental Causes for Physical Illness and the Way to Overcome Them.* Carlsbad, CA: Hay House, 1998.

Make of it what you will. I consult the book because I'm convinced health problems do have human causes. When my father was dying early in 2007, I had a case of bronchitis that developed into several other problems because I had an antibiotic-resistant strain of bacteria in me. I consulted the book then. Under "lung problems," Hay lists "depression and grief" as her first two causes. I was experiencing both those things—I was available for bacteria to invade.

ABOUT MAKING FACES

There is a lot about Paul Ekman's (and his research associates') work on the www. Ekman has a website: www.paulekman.com that is worth reading. Ekman has also published several books. You will find them listed on the website. I have not yet read Ekman's books (I will eventually, he's on my list); I have read about him and his work and I have read many of the articles on the website. We all read faces to some degree but Ekman and his associates have made a very useful science of it.

Gladwell, Malcolm. *Blink: The Power of Thinking Without Thinking.* New York: Back Bay Books, 2007.

The book is about a much larger subject than just the faces we make, and Gladwell is a wonderful writer. The reason it is listed here is that Gladwell includes a section on Paul Ekman's work in the book.

Shamanic Soul Retrieval and a Digression About "The Knock of the Spirit"

IN SHAMANIC TRADITIONS worldwide there is a practice called "soul retrieval." Though often widely separated geographically, these various shamanic traditions are consistently ancient, and astonishingly consistent in how they work, and in what a shaman can or cannot do within them. They are traditions that are still practiced in places where the Age of Reason (and the subsequent re-visioning of the world as somehow mechanical) did not get a stranglehold on people's minds and on the process of education; or they are revivals of the older traditions. The idea of soul retrieval is common to them all.

Before I'm dismissed entirely for taking potshots at reason, I should remind the reader that for me, beginning with the spider business, the last few years have opened some new—or very old—ideas to possibility. There was, for me, a single moment that started the new learning: it was when the Reiki practitioner made the pain of the spider-bite wound go away by putting his hand over it. There were some months when I wouldn't even talk about that experience (opprobrium is strong stuff), and there are still moments when somebody looks at me like my lid has flipped because I had that experience at all.

I risked credibility by opening this book with the spider story. There are people who (if they even get this far) will dismiss the ideas because I claim the events of that story as my experience. It is my experience. At the time, it was rather scary. It felt like a gap in what is real opened in front of me when that man turned from the coffeepot and asked what I had to do with Hopi mythology, and I remembered what I had done just a few weeks before with the key-ring image of Kokopelli in an art gallery in Steamboat Springs, Colorado.

And then—heads up!—the spider mythology, Spider as the keeper of language and stories, Spider's plans . . . Never mind what had happened so recently on the massage table; I was already an old hand at having people find things on my body that they couldn't see with their eyes and I hadn't revealed to them.

So my question became this: am I so imprisoned by my habitual perceiving and thinking that something new (or old) can't be possible? It is a good question. Another good question: who decides what is true, what isn't, and when? Is it those sneaky memes again? Maybe it is. We are certainly trained in what the culture we are born to believes from the instant we take our first breath in the world. And anything that doesn't fit that worldview, we are supposed to ignore or forget, and sometimes we are even punished if we don't forget quickly enough. For instance: there are stories, in cultures that believe in reincarnation, of children who can sometimes even remember where they lived and who they lived with in a previous life, and can sometimes even name and find those people. My mama didn't teach me that. Or, much more mundane, how about knowing sometimes who is calling before you pick up the phone, and I don't mean knowing with the help of caller ID? Or having a dream that is predictive of events that happen? Or, even just having dreams with real meaning in our lives? Mostly, we give up these knowings, or we risk being labeled crazy. Or unstable. Or just plain vanilla *odd* (fine old word, "odd," came to its current use in Middle English from the Norse).

Ok. Odd. Here's the dream that came to me in the eighteen hours of sleep recounted in my spider story, the sleep I was busy doing when the dog messed in the house . . . In the dream, I was part bear somehow, I was heavy and fur-covered and I had a snout that I looked down to see, and I was held by my leg to a big post, like a telephone pole, by a cuff and heavy chain. A creature that was part human and part something else was eating me alive. A portion of an arm (a foreleg, in this case) and whole back leg were already gone from me, the creature kept coming back, taking huge chunks and, each time, more of me was missing. I was terrified, in great pain, bleeding, dying, and furious beyond description. (Yep, rage.) I was unable to get loose from the post. I was a prisoner of the thing that was eating me. And there came a moment when I had to laugh at the absurdity my own demise: I, Jo, in some sort of strange bear getup, was being eaten alive! And when I began to laugh, even with just a first derisive snort, the creature could not eat any more of me. It could not come close to me if I was really laughing, and the more I laughed, the less of me was missing, and then I laughed great belly laughs, and I had the belly of a bear to do it with, I laughed until I was no longer chained to the post and I could move away. In the dream, I did.

There is nothing in this world like night school.

There are cultures (Native American, assorted African and Aboriginal, to name a few) in which dreams are valued and studied, and even children are encouraged to recount their dreams from the time they can talk because "true dreaming" begins as a child, and true dreaming is nurtured and thought useful to the community. These cultures value true dreamers, they listen to them. True dreamers are thought to have access to wisdom and crazy wisdom and sometimes access to what we think of—because of our perception of time—as the future, and other really interesting realms of knowledge like healing or distance-seeing. So a true dreamer is also considered to be a potential healer but the dreaming is valued for itself. We are, all of us, capable of true dreaming. Some of us are just more fluent in the language of the dream than others. I had—heads up!—a healing dream.

I am still learning from it.

We use somewhere (I've read different numbers, and the specific number doesn't really matter, it is the magnitude that is important) between ten percent and twenty percent of our brain's capacity during our waking consciousness. Even if that number were fifty percent (it is not nearly that high), what is the other fifty percent of our brain for, and when and how did we come not to use it?

Let me reframe this into a different possibility: let's say that we do use our whole brain, we just don't understand all the use, we only understand somewhere around twenty percent of it, and we're still learning how to process *most* of the information our brains receive. Makes a person feel a little different about the possibilities, doesn't it?

Imagine this: you are lying with your face part way through what looks like a little padded toilet seat which is the head support on a massage table; imagine yourself with a hole the size of a fifty-cent piece in your lower back that goes all the way through the flesh to the pelvic bone. The hole started growing in the first couple of days you had it; it grew from a place that hurt like a burn about the size of a dime to a place the size of an old silver dollar that really hurt. Now, when you look at it in the mornings (that's when sunlight comes in the bathroom window), you are twisted around to see your rear end in the mirror. The twisting hurts, but most everything hurts right now. You can see what you suspect is your pelvic bone in the hole. Now imagine keeping the hole salted really thoroughly all the time. Imagine feeling foolish. "You have what? Where?" And hurting a lot at the same time. Imagine fear, too. If this thing gets into your spine, if it destroys those nerves, you will really have some trouble, like not being able to walk, so you keep putting on more salt, nitroglycerin, to force the blood to flow and keep this hole from getting any bigger, and to keep it from getting necrotic. The nitro makes you pass out sometimes when you put it on, but you are afraid not to put it on, so you put it on lying down so you won't fall when you pass out. (You learned this the hard way and three weeks later, you still have a very sore place on your head to remind you.)

Now, imagine walking into a stranger's house. You've been talked into coming here, you really didn't feel like coming, but here you are, your little misery very, very close behind. Six people are standing around a massage table set up in a living room.

What they are doing looks stupid: they just stand there and put their hands on people. Somebody lies down on the massage table, everybody else puts their hands on him, and nothing happens. They all just stand there. When it is your turn, you climb onto the table. You think, "I'm wearing polyester. It is not natural, it probably makes a difference, I should go home." Now imagine an engineer who works at one of the larger chemical plants in the state. He's wearing a sweatshirt that says he "hearts" higher math, and he's standing beside your butt in the circle around the table, and after a moment, he asks, "What is this?" You lift your head and crane your neck around to see who he is and where. It is then you notice the sweatshirt. His hand is over your body, not even touching your unnatural fleece yet, just over the soon-to-be-holy hole in your back, and you return your face to the little toilet seat and say to the floor, "It's a spider bite, a brown recluse." Nothing has happened yet. Not to you. You can think (I did), "That's odd," but nothing has happened to you yet. Then the people put their hands on you. The engineer puts one of his hands directly over the wound on your body, over the fleece, and the hand gets very warm—well, something does happen after all—and the pain begins to go away. Imagine doubting yourself, wondering if the pain is really going away, wondering what the pain is, if it can be made to go away like that. Imagine the pain lessening by degrees over the course of two or three minutes, like the engineer was somehow pulling the pain out of the hole with his hot hand. Imagine lying there, looking at the floor, seeing the feet and slender lower legs of the person who has her hands on your head, feeling the pain going away, and, finally, feeling the absence of pain.

Something *has* happened now, and it has happened to you.

The moment is called "the knock of the spirit." I don't know where the naming came from (maybe Castaneda, don Juan does use the phrase), but its use is common in my experience, and it refers to a change of perception that occurs in the moment. It is often a moment in which someone is cognizant with more than just the rational mind—call it gut-level cognizant (butt-level cognizant in my case), body learning, cognizant that something new has happened. Feel: it is not an intellectual exercise on the Reiki table. Someone is suddenly cognizant that the world may not work the way he or she had always assumed it did. There is now a choice. The choice is to ignore the moment, dismiss it, set out to forget it. Or to pursue it. I asked, "How did you do that?" And then, I followed where the question led.

The pain in the spider wound did not stay gone, and I kept going back for more Reiki. Reiki took the pain away again every time I went. But the nitroglycerin always made it come back. In the meantime, I had more interesting things to read than murder mysteries. When I asked my big question, "How did you do that?" I was offered some books. (You will find those and more listed in the Further Practice sections of this book.)

I see what I do with the story work in a new way now because I followed that lead. I live with a different perception than the one I lived with when I first started working with communities and their stories. It was the one I had lived with for most of my life, the one I lived with until that knock.* I saw some of the changes that individuals and communities experienced before my perception change, but I didn't see the possible why(s) or how(s). The study, the learning since, and the people who have contributed to my learning are a wonder and a pleasure, but it was that knock, the "knock-up-the-side-of-the-head-with-a-two-by-four" (my shaman friend, an incorrigible punster, says "a two-by-meta-phor"), that began it.

My shaman friend's "knock of the spirit" was a lightning strike he barely lived through that arrived while he was sitting in a hot tub in Gatlinburg, Tennessee. Until that time, he'd designed water parks. "Lightning changes you from 110 volts to 220," he says (another joke, in his telling) but the learning was not the least bit easy and began with a voice that made him question whether he was still sane or not. And lightning strikes are never a joke. On the other hand, there were shamans-in-training in Native American traditions who sought out opportunities for lightning strikes or near strikes and if they lived through it . . . This man really does channel a lot of energy with his hands. They feel electric.

Another knock story, about the woman who was scalped in a car wreck and had a near-death experience, is recounted previously in The Asterisks section of the "Physical Keeping of

Emotion" chapter. Another knock story from another energy healer tells of his going blind and literally stumbling into a Reiki master (he fell onto her). Fifteen years after going blind, he has a license to drive again with no traditional medical involvement in the healing. Yet another is of an M.D. who had a pain in her neck she couldn't medicate away until someone suggested a shiatsu practitioner who could and did take care of the problem, and that same big question—"How did you do that?"—led the M.D. to Sufi teaching and an energy practice that complements her traditional medical practice. I am fascinated with knock stories. Some are certainly knocked harder than others, but they all recount the moments when perception opens a little and a person's paradigm begins to shift. My knock story: I got a spider bite and went for Reiki. I'm truly grateful I didn't get struck by lightning, didn't go blind, didn't get scalped. I got a spider bite, and a guy who "hearts" higher math could make the pain go away.

The reading and study and experience that have followed my knock have allowed me to begin to think and write about the energy in what was once simply "the work I do for a living." The story work (with communities) is now more than just what I do for a living: it is bigger than I understood at first. Our stories define our lives, and how we think about and tell our stories make a huge difference in the quality of our lives. Any shaman in the world will tell you that.

Western medicine and religion have been very quick to name shamanism as valueless superstition. That is changing. I had morning TV on in a motel room in one of the communities where I was working, and there was an interview on *The Today Show* with an M.D. who uses a bear mask and healing dances with his patients. I found the use of the bear interesting because bear as a totem, as an energetic power, is about unlocking the power of the subconscious, and if you can access the subconscious (read, among other things, "if you can get beyond your own monkey mind"), your body can often heal itself.

Some new-age folks have been quick to claim old skills whether they have them or not so there is definitely some snake oil in the territory, but traditional shamanism is not just superstition enlarged to belief. It can and does work as a healing system. I understand what a heretic I sound like (again), and I swear I am not advocating doing away with allopathic medicine. By all means if you break an arm, or rupture an appendix, or get a snake bite, go allopathic. A doctor can set your bone, give you pain meds, cut out your appendix, and shoot you up with antitoxin. Good stuff. If you are sick from anything except direct environmental causes, go to a healer *and* a doctor. If your dis-ease stems from your environment, go to a healer, a doctor *and* a bulldog lawyer. Listen to the healer when he or she talks about the cause of illness and how to let the energy of it go. A medical intuitive can often speak about the energy of an illness, and what the causes of it might be. Many Reiki people can do the same. A Sufi healer can often do the same. The information is literally held in the energy around our bodies, which is part of our being, and there are people who can read and understand that information. There are doctors who can do something similar, not that it is taught (yet) in medical school. They do it by bringing empathy and experience to the science.

In the meantime, with the intent of expanding human use of the gray matter, listen to your dreams. They really do talk to you. Dreams that name or pinpoint health troubles before they are diagnosed are called "prodromal dreams," and they are actually pretty common.

A story that haunts me took place when whites brought smallpox to this country and it began decimating native peoples. This is the Cherokee version of a common story. The disease killed about half the Real People in a first (recorded) encounter in 1738. It was something their healers couldn't do anything about (Western medicine still cannot stop a virus once it gets inside a person). They'd never dealt with anything like it before; they felt their ancient sources of power and healing had deserted them; and if the gods had deserted the Real People, the shaman's traditional tools (songs, chants, herbs, etc.) no longer had any value. Many destroyed their equipment and sacred objects, and in some cases they destroyed themselves as well. There is a parallel to this story happening now: many sources of power aren't even possibilities for most of us, we've thrown them away.

The shamanic idea of soul retrieval says that during hard events or painful events or very fearful events in our lives, pieces of our "soul" (I'd say "energy") are sometimes left behind, literally separated from the rest of us, and left in that time and place where the event happened. This loss of soul or energy can cause dis-function and dis-comfort, even illness. What a shaman does is reach through time and space to pick up the lost pieces and return them to the individual and help restore his or her health.

Remember the neuropeptides held in our tissue and the practice of shiatsu that helps release them. Remember the constrictions in the energy body made by memory and reinforced by monkey mind. Remember that these places can literally be found by a practitioner who can feel or see energy. These things are all as real as the nose on your face. You just can't see them without some practice. The irony is that collecting personal energy, no longer giving your own energy to old pain is what allows you to become cognizant of another's energy. (It also takes practice.) Seeing or feeling another's energy is sometimes a matter of having enough of your own to do it. And recovering energy from things that have usurped it, this soul retrieval, is one way to go about it.

Toltec (energy) tradition teaches the same idea as soul retrieval (that our energy is left with people and events in our lives), but Toltecs practice a different way of recovering that energy: it is called recapitulation and the term is connotative of the technique. It is complicated and can be challenging, but it can be done by an individual. It does not take a shaman's active participation to achieve value from it.

Buddhist tradition teaches that until we let go and forgive old events, we are still giving energy to them, we are "caught in illusion." Buddhist practice does not speak (to my knowledge) of retrieving energy left behind, except that in the moment we cease to give energy to old pain, we have more of the energy for other things.

Neurolinguistic programming teaches a "timeline therapy." The idea is that our perspective on the events of our lives changes as we grow older, and the adult can give the child they once were a new understanding of events. NLP says the child can come forward in time with this new understanding. Psychology's work with the "wounded child" has some of the same effect. Neither of these processes talks about what happens in energy terms, and neither speaks specifically of returning the energy (or soul) left with the old events, but what is accomplished by both of them is that a person can quit pouring current energy into old pain.

Reframing an experience for an individual is another way for a person to be able to stop giving energy to old events.

But the larger idea of soul retrieval is more than just ceasing to give energy away. A shaman, in an astral body or an energy body or a dreaming body travels into some kind of continuum in which time is nonlinear, a quantum time where everything is happening in the same huge moment in what is now considered to be one (or more) of at least eleven (or maybe as many as twenty-three, says string theory) dimensions. The shaman picks up the pieces of soul (energy) that the patient left somewhere else, comes back, and delivers those pieces to the sick patient and the patient gets well. Or he delivers pieces of soul back to a depressed patient, and the depression goes away. Or he returns a piece of soul, and a painful joint works again. Or, he returns a piece of soul and a patient can quit smoking or drinking because the need is no longer there. The list goes on.

It works better than you might think.

In my story work, when I add the passage past a dragon or reframe an event so it no longer has the same pain (find the meaning, relieve the pain), the person whose story it is can stop giving energy to that old event.**

But more happens with the public performance of a hard story. It is a parallel of soul retrieval. We are putting someone onstage as a personification of the person to whom the story happened; sometimes we are even putting the person whose story it is onstage. We are not changing the event, but we are adding a passage past a dragon or reframing it so the event has value beyond just pain. We are pulling events from the past into the present transformed. And, then, we reinforce the transformation in a series of rehearsals and performances.

In Huna (a Hawaiian traditional shamanic energy practice, and I'm not doing anything near justice to the tradition or the practice with this note), there is a funny technique that works: if you stub your toe, make the gesture a few more times without going all the way to impact, and you will, in the moments of repeating the gesture, retrain the brain to see the gesture as meaning something besides the pain, and the stubbed toe will hurt less and heal quicker. Reenacting or telling a reframed event onstage, rehearsing and then repeating it in public performance however many times, is the same idea.

Are we having fun yet?

⊰ THE ASTERISKS ⊱

*There have been other knocks on my perception but I didn't recognize them as such, or maybe they were setups for the knock that worked. My writing life is blessed with synchronicities, the largest and most amazing of which was Bear #75. He was a big (close to five hundred pounds), very much alive black bear who had been numbered and moved from Cades Cove in Great Smoky Mountains National Park because he was a troublesome bear, and he was on his way home when he showed up at my back door in the middle of Johnson City, Tennessee, a town of fifty-thousand-plus. He came when I was writing a play (one of my own, not a community piece) called *The Bear Facts*. I was stuck in it, I didn't know where to go next because it seemed to have a bear—this one #100 for reasons of her own—who was a character in it, and I didn't know how to do that. I didn't know how I could make that work. I'd been piddling for weeks, worrying, not writing, when Bear #75 showed up on the other side of my kitchen screen door and looked in at me. He'd come through some chain-link fences to get there, he was not at my back door by the path of least resistance. He stayed for two or three minutes, but it felt like an eternity. My father was at my house and he, too, saw the bear. We saw the bear, smelled the bear, felt the wildness in the presence of the bear. I felt more than the wild if that is possible. I understood the synchronicity in that moment. I was in awe and that transcendence of time and space that is synchronicity. Is it happening to me yet? Well, yes.

I didn't quit working on the play, I wrote a bear. The first word she said in my script was: "*MOVE!*"

I did start reading about synchronicity (significant coincidence, what words those are!) and about bears and human relationships to bears. Now, some years since Bear #75 appeared at my door, I still see more bears in the mountains when I'm riding my horse than others who have been riding much longer or more often than I. These sightings feel like ongoing gifts.

I also know (now) to pay special attention to dreams that have bears in them. They are always big, vivid dreams. How can I not pay attention? The bear dreams that have come still have huge resonances in me and I can call up images and feelings from them instantly. The bear dreams tell me about my state of being. I am (so far) a bear in them. And because those dreams have been so big, I started trying to learn about dreams. This is a huge return for having tried to write a bear (giving agency to a bear?), or maybe I had to write a bear to find one.

From all this, I know (at least a little) about what it means to have a totem with *meaning* in my life, and a very real sense that more of this world is connected than I understand.

One more bear dream. This one came about three months after the chained-to-the-post bear dream (recounted previously), and a couple of weeks after a brief bout in a hospital with hyperthyroid troubles and my shaman friend's naming of rage as a problem for me. I took the dream as a progress report. In it, I am somehow bear again, and a creature (feels like the same one but no part of it is human this time) is after me. I am not chained, but I cannot escape just by moving away, it chases me, grabs me with its teeth and holds on. I drag it with me, my flesh is torn and I hurt. It does not quit. And there comes a moment in the dream when I have had enough of it. I take the thing in my mouth, because a mouth is what I have, and I jerk it from where it has its teeth sunk in my side. I rip another hole in myself but I do not care. I eviscerate it with my claws, and I eat it, bones and skin, skull and claws. I eat it all. I lick the blood from my forepaws. And then I wake up.

And one more real bear story. This is another layer in the synchronicities around Bear #75's visit to my door, and the play *The Bear Facts*. Bear #75 was shot with a tranquilizer shortly after he left my kitchen door, loaded onto a truck and moved to Roan Mountain, released, and the next day shot and killed close to Flag Pond, Tennessee, by someone trying to take a trophy. His story and his number appeared in the newspaper. That was when I learned that he, like the bear I wanted to write, was a numbered bear.

I cried for him, for the waste of killing him. And I dedicated the play to him, seemed like the least I could do: "For Bear #75." And I tell the portion I know of his story in honor of him.

Some years later, Barter Theatre in Abingdon, Virginia, decided to produce *The Bear Facts*. I had to be in Newport News, Virginia, on the other side of the state so I was not able to be where I wanted to be, at rehearsal in Abingdon. I always take books when I'm traveling because experience in a motel room is closer to tolerable with something good to read. I took three or four books from my bedside stack, and included was a little book I had bought months before but had not opened. It was way down in the stack, I had to look for it to include it in my luggage. It was *Black Bear Reflections* by Ken Jenkins. It is a small book, mostly pictures (Jenkins is a photographer) of black bears in Great Smoky Mountains National Park. I took it with me as a gesture in honor of bear spirit. I wanted a gesture of some kind, since I couldn't be at rehearsal. The afternoon rehearsals started at Barter Theatre, on the other side of Virginia, I picked up the book and thumbed through it. A few pages from the end of the book, there was a picture of the bear who came to my door and his story. Bear #75 showed up again, for me, in a motel room in Newport News, as the play dedicated to him began rehearsal elsewhere. It was almost as shocking and wondrous as his huge smelly presence at my kitchen door those years before, and it certainly qualified as another significant coincidence for me, one of a series that felt magical to say the least. Yes, I made the opportunity for it, I took the book with me to Newport News. I thumbed through the book at the right time. But I didn't know my mentor bear was in the book till I saw him looking back at me from his picture.

Significant coincidence, but only for me. Seeing the bear's picture wouldn't have mattered the same way to anybody else. Synchronicity is almost always a personal event.

⊰⊱

**Other story notes (a shallow dip in deep stuff).

1. Jerome Bruner (he's so quotable) says "an individual who has lost the ability to construct narrative has lost himself." (Oliver Sacks wrote about such a patient in *The Man Who Mistook His Wife for a Hat*.) Humans make stories. It is part of what makes us human. You and I have to make narrative to do something so simple as make coffee. This, this, then this . . . narrative. Imagine losing that. You can't do it. You have to make narrative in order to imagine losing it.

More–humans are designed to learn from other humans via story (narrative). Telling and listening (teller and witness) are both tremendously important for an individual, a family and a community. It is an argument–if one was needed beyond the ongoing support of itinerant playwrights–for doing the story plays.

Jerome Bruner, again: "Stories define self and other." It is another big idea, and I'll take it further. We define ourselves by the stories we tell about ourselves *to ourselves and to others*. They may be different stories but, often, they are different versions of the same story. So there are public and private selves that are also defined by stories. And, to reiterate, when we tell the harder stories to ourselves (or to others) without a passage past a dragon or a reframing, we are putting the same chemistry back into our bodies, and so doing the same thing to our energy that the original event did. We are still giving energy to the past and reinforcing a pattern in our being, not changing it. Keeping a hard story private while some whitewash of the same story becomes the public version can be a rather schizoid way to try to live. At the least, it is a lie with its assorted tangled webs. Lies are often fear-based, we tell them for fear of something else, and fear does essentially the same thing in the body's energy as anger. (There is, obviously, a level of magnitude here: white lies are often social grease, and making a lie of a speeding ticket or a co-worker's hairdo is not the same as, for instance, making a lie of something felt in the body as a betrayal.) What is important is that a successful passage past a dragon or a reframing of experience that has value for the individual (or a community) cannot be an emotional lie. In my story work, this means that in the reframing of a story, I can take it beyond what I know to be factual; I just cannot take it beyond what *feels* like it could be true. The trick word in that sentence is *feels*, and therein lies the art for any who would go about story work of any kind.

I wish I could say that I thought the stories we tell to others are stories in which we have already found some value. For some of us (and some of our stories) that may be true, but I don't think it is very often. Just listen—ok, eavesdrop, you have my permission—and observe. Remember that you can see in the teller's face what a story feels like. Most stories we tell are stories that reinforce energetic patterns that are already there, and we aren't the least bit aware of it. Stories between us are what make close friends or mates, and we do look to the people we trust to help make sense of the events of our lives; that is a process of story-making. Friends or families or support groups that simply reinforce a wounded identity in the process (and do no more) are an energetic disaster.

Story-making/sense-making take on another level of urgency with those who are ill. Serious illness demands story, if for no other reason than to address the "Why me?" question in it. Allopathic medicine has been inclined to separate body and mind/being and focus on the body pretty exclusively. But the being that inhabits body has to have, and will make, story. A person can find himself with a broken story because of illness. A person who finds himself really sick must reinvent a self that accommodates an uncomfortable, sometimes life-threatening and, usually though not always, unanticipated debilitation. The new story he makes will have a lot to do with his chances of survival.

2. Most of the mystical traditions teach that you have to literally give up your personal history to truly succeed (achieve enlightenment). Talk about cleaning up energy. Say, "I have no past," and live as if it were true. Even if you want to do it, it would be very hard.

No spider bite . . . Who would I be without that experience?

Some of the practices that help the "no past" endeavor are interesting to try. One is to break habits. Habits are another kind of story in our lives. Sleep in a different place occasionally, and even when you do sleep in your bed, don't sleep in the same direction all the time. Put your shoes on in a different order from the usual. Uncross your legs. Put your belt through the loops in the opposite direction. Drink tea instead of coffee sometimes. Don't plan it, just do it in the moment. A little practice at this, and you will find that almost *everything* is done with habit behind it and when you start breaking those habits, you make room for another kind of reframing, a physical one.

Habits of thinking are the same song, second verse to physical habits. I know about this specific endeavor from energy work and from theater. Try this: find some way to say yes to everything. (Malcolm Gladwell describes this "yes" business as the single rule of an improvisational theater company in his book *Blink*.) I suggest trying to do this for a day or two at a time. You don't have to do things against who or what you are, but instead of saying, "I can't do that," try stating it in a positive way, "What a *good* way to turn me into a screaming meemie!" One of the energy healers (Barbara Brennan) obliges her students to accept every opportunity they are offered for a solid week. This does not sound like much until you try to do it. The "yes" business is, for most of us, a radical shift in awareness because "no" is such an automatic response (a habit) in most of us that we are not even aware of it. You open yourself to possibility (a big don Juan lesson) by following a "yes" in ways that are hard to imagine unless you try it.

3. Don Juan gave Carlos Castaneda an assignment; *The Active Side of Infinity* is the book he produced out of it. The assignment, as I understand it, was to find/remember those things or moments in his life that had shaped him, shaped his thinking, or caused a change in his path, and to tell those stories. The changes are sometimes not even conscious choices, often they come about because of someone else's action, and they are rarely the stories we usually tell about ourselves. I've been playing with this assignment.

Finding the moments of genuine change is not easy and it's sometimes rather uncomfortable. For instance: I am a writer now because, at age thirty-something, I got rejected for a job I really wanted as an actor, and after a lot of significant gestures—yelling, weeping and gnashing of teeth, etc.—I applied myself to the new business at hand and was soon making a (modest) living at it, something I'd not managed to do as an actor. I wasn't even a decent actor. I had a lot of trouble with something as basic to the art as remembering lines. I see that event now as the most fortuitous rejection of my life thus far, but it didn't feel that way at the time. Looking at it from some distance has allowed me to reframe it. Another big-change moment: my mother, ill with Alzheimer's, looked at me and said, "I don't know you, who are you?" and I realized how lost to me she was. I knew then that no matter how long her body lived, I would not have my mother again in this life. I let her go then. It did not change the duty of care-giving, but it made the work a job, not a nightmare; and her death, when it finally came, was a release, not a loss. These were both sea changes in my being but I didn't see them as such at the time. What kind of bucket was I wearing on my head? A bucket o' memes, I reckon.

Another big event: I stood in that art gallery in Steamboat Springs, Colorado, and asked a Trickster for change with my heart in the request. I called this one to me. I do not recommend what I did as a good thing to do; I don't even recommend it as a way to wake up. The change has been hard ("You're not dying, this is just a heads-up!") and dangerous (people can lose limbs or die of brown recluse bites), and some of it certainly has not been what I thought I wanted (like the end of the love affair), but the change is ongoing and astonishing. And worth every bit of what it cost.

4. Oral history interviews can be a demonstration of how the web of memory works. An interviewee can find himself telling stories he had "forgotten" for whatever reasons. "Oh, I hadn't thought of that in years . . ." is a common line in transcripts.

Judging from the oral histories I have read (hundreds of them), I don't think it happens very often, but sharing experiences in a story circle can go some distance toward a reframing of those stories. An oral history from Harlan, Kentucky, is an example of that. The document comes from a story circle about floods, living through floods, living in a place that often floods. Some of these were very hard stories. Over the course of the telling among five or six people, the feeling emerges that the floods were hard and dangerous, but they were also fun: families drew close during the floods, people worked together and helped each other. "A rich man runs from rising water same way a poor one does." The man who ran the story circle said, at one point (I'm paraphrasing), "I never thought I'd say this, but it sounds like we could use a good flood around here." And the people at the table laughed and agreed. The rest of the transcript became about all the fun they had had during floods.

Further Practice

ABOUT BEAR

Jenkins, Ken. *Black Bear Reflections*. Merrillville, IN: ICS Books, 1995.

You'll find part of Bear #75's story on page 51. And you'll find a photo of the bear himself. He was a big, magnificent bear.

Rockwell, David B. *Giving Voice to Bear: American Indian Myths, Rituals, and Images of the Bear*. Lanham, MD: Roberts Rinehart, 2003.

Great book, amazing pictures.

Shepard, Paul and Barry Sanders. *The Sacred Paw: The Bear in Nature, Myth, and Literature*. New York: Viking, 1985.

Bears have been big in human imagination for a very long time. This book covers it.

ABOUT DREAMS

Barasch, Marc Ian. *Healing Dreams: Exploring the Dreams That Can Transform Your Life*. New York: Riverhead Books, 2000.

I started paying real attention to my dreams after I read this book.

Cayce, Edgar.

Jess Stern and others have written about Cayce's work; I've sampled a lot of the writing. Cayce is famous because he was so often right. (Try rubbing peanut oil on your skin for joint troubles like arthritis or try a warm castor oil pack to reduce swelling.) You can find more information by Googling "peanut oil" or "castor oil" and checking the Cayce references, but that's hardly a beginning on Cayce's work. My reason for listing Cayce under "About Dreams" is that he literally slept to access knowledge. The work of Cayce's Association for Research and Enlightenment (A.R.E.) is ongoing: www.edgarcayce.org

ABOUT HANDS-ON HEALING/REIKI

Gordon, Richard. *Quantum-Touch: The Power to Heal.* Berkeley, CA: North Atlantic Books, 2006.

This is a how-to book, not traditional Reiki, but *QT* teaches the same thing. The book includes some thinking that is useful about how hands-on healing works (resonance).

Stein, Diane. *Essential Reiki: A Complete Guide to an Ancient Healing Art.* Freedom, CA: Crossing Press, 1995.

This is a how-to manual for people who have done (or are interested in doing) the traditional Reiki attunements. Stein raised a lot of hackles among traditional practitioners when she published this book because she published symbols and other "secrets."

ABOUT HUNA

Long, Max Freedom. *The Secret Science Behind Miracles.* Los Angeles: Huna Research Publications, 1954.

This is a white man writing about native tradition early in the twentieth century, but with more respect than that usually implies. This is, if you read it right, a how-to book. Huna thinking found the subconscious long before Freud or Jung ever thought of it.

ABOUT OUT-OF-THE-BODY WORK

Monroe, Robert A. *Journeys Out of the Body.* Garden City, NY: Doubleday, 1971.

Monroe was a middle-aged businessman when he began to understand the naps he took were sometimes a little out of the ordinary. The work of the Monroe Institute is ongoing (www.monroeinstitute.com). A lot of the Monroe Institute's work is with sound, and their Hemi-Sync technology CDs are the easiest way I know to balance both sides of the brain. Meditation will get you to the same place, just takes longer to learn.

ABOUT REINCARNATION

Shroder, Thomas. *Old Souls: The Scientific Evidence for Past Lives.* New York: Simon & Schuster, 1999.

This man was a doubter, he started the search he recounts to disprove reincarnation.

ABOUT SHAMANISM

Harner, Michael J. *The Way of the Shaman: A Guide to Power and Healing.* San Francisco: Harper & Row, 1980.

This is usually the first resource recommended on the subject of shamanism, something of a how-to book. This is also beginning thinking and Harner is a respected anthropologist with experience to back up what he has to say.

Villoldo, Ph.D., Alberto and Stanley Krippner, Ph. D. *Healing States: A Journey into the World of Spiritual Healing and Shamanism.* New York: Simon & Schuster, 1987.

(See Vitebsky below.)

Vitebsky, Piers. *The Shaman.* Boston: Little, Brown & Company, 1995.

I've done a lot of reading on the subject of shamanism; to me, both this book and the one by Villoldo/Krippner don't seem to be snake oil.

ABOUT SYNCHRONICITY

Combs, Allan and Mark Holland. *Synchronicity: Science, Myth, and the Trickster.* New York: Marlow & Co., 1996.

This book takes a big interesting bite. Knowing something about the science of Chaos and the Trickster tradition before you read it helps.

Hopcke, Robert H. *There Are No Accidents: Synchronicity and the Stories of Our Lives.* New York: Riverhead Books, 1997.

Start reading here.

Jung, Carl G. *Synchronicity: An Acausal Connecting Principle.* New York: Routledge, 1985.

This is early thinking about synchronicity; Jung noticed, maybe named, synchronicity and discussed how it worked. He didn't have the science of Chaos to draw on when he wrote this work. I wish he had. I'd love to see what he'd have to say with that addition.

THINKING FROM THE ACADEMY ABOUT STORIES IN OUR LIVES

There has been a tremendous amount of work done on stories, the human inclination to make stories, and the development of the brain as a story-maker. I've sampled some of this in my omnivorous reading, though I cannot say I've studied the field. You'll find faint echoes of the work of Jerome Bruner and Dan P. McAdams in the asterisks above. None of what I've read in the traditional thinking about stories and story-making, myth-making, agency, any of it, has explored an energy application to the stories of our lives. So this book is not part of a measurable science (yet) or even accepted thinking by the stretch of any imagination except my own: I'm sailing uncharted water. These references are a limited sampling of the better charted waters. Most of these folks come from the discipline of psychology.

Bruner, Jerome. *Actual Minds, Possible Worlds.* Cambridge, MA: Harvard University Press, 1986.

_____. *Making Stories: Law, Literature, Life.* New York: Farrar, Straus & Giroux, 2002.

This man is a wonderful writer.

Frank, Arthur W. *The Wounded Storyteller: Body, Illness, and Ethics.* Chicago: University of Chicago Press, 1995.

Dealing with illness, mostly theory. Useful "sick" reading.

Goffman, Erving. *The Presentation of Self in Everyday Life.* London: Allen Lane, 1969.

This is the big daddy of traditional thinking; he is behind a lot of the thinking that has become the academic tradition. This is just one of his many books.

Kleinman, M.D., Arthur. *The Illness Narratives: Suffering, Healing, & the Human Condition.* New York: Basic Books, 1988.

Like the Frank book, this is useful "sick" reading.

Lakoff, George and Mark Johnson. *Metaphors We Live By.* Chicago: University of Chicago Press, 1980.

Metaphors are magic.

McAdams, Dan P. *The Stories We Live By: Personal Myths and the Making of the Self.* New York: William Morrow & Company, 1993.

This is the second time I've listed this book, he belongs here too.

The Holographic Model of the Brain and the Universe

THE NEXT IDEA: take the holographic process as a model (a model, not a literal description) for the mind and then, if you care to take it further, let the model serve for the whole of the universe.

A hologram is a photograph in three dimensions. If we made a hologram of an orange and then projected it, it would look as if a real orange had appeared in the air in front of our eyes. Holography—the way to make that picture—is a lensless photography in which waves of light, one from a direct source and a second reflected from the object being photographed are captured on a photographic plate as an interference pattern. Imagine two stones dropped in a still pond at the same time in different places: the pattern created where the waves meet is an interference pattern. The photographic plate holding the image seems to be a meaningless pattern of swirls until it is placed in a coherent light beam, a laser, then the original wave pattern is remade and a three-dimensional image of the orange we photographed is projected. Our orange appears in front of us.

According to neuroscientist Karl Pribram, memory is not held in just one place in the brain; rather, it is spread throughout the brain. In other words, it is not just one memory here, another over there. Each memory is spread through the brain like the waves from a stone dropped in a pond. Since we have more than one memory, we have a series of these waves that meet and develop interference patterns and then spread through the whole of the brain like the photographic plate that captures interference patterns in a hologram. One of the oddities of a hologram is that the plate with our orange on it can be broken and our whole orange can still be projected (with the laser) from any part of the plate that is left. This is also true of your brain: losing some part of the brain does not necessarily mean a specific memory is lost. It can be re-created from other parts of the brain. This is part of why Karl Pribram finds the holographic model so appropriate. The big difference—it is obvious, but I'll point it out anyway—is that the photographic plate is fixed; the living brain is dynamic.

I'm interested in this because it means that our memories have relationships to each other. Our memories have their own interference patterns. One memory can call another and another and another . . . The line I see so often in story collections, "Oh, I hadn't thought of that in years!" is indicative of these interference patterns in memory in a very basic and self-evident way. These relationships become especially important in the context of monkey mind when one memory can and does call another and another. When a hard story gets a reframe or a passage past the dragon, it is going to change the interference patterns in the brain of the person who holds that story. It will change the story's connections to other stories in that person's memory. This carries a possibility for the person whose memory it is: a story that has new meaning will no longer call up other previously connected hard stories in the same way, or, even better, the other hard stories will open themselves to a reframing in light of the new thinking about the first story. This is called learning from experience, but the holographic model is an interesting way to think about the process. In our culture, it has some other references, too. "Benefiting from therapy" is one of them.

Now, for that holographic universe, try this: remember, first, that if a holographic plate is broken, the whole image can be reconstructed from any piece of it. The whole is reflected in all its parts. To play with the possibilities of this: a single atom of matter looks rather like our solar system (and maybe works like it too; maybe weak and strong atomic forces and gravity are part of another energetic "family" like the electromagnetic spectrum. Current thinking says they are, says that they are products of the zero point field). So maybe this Earth is an electron in an atom of matter (our solar system) which is part of a molecule (our galaxy) which is part of the heart of a CEO (our universe) who is making a financial killing in some cosmic equivalent of solar technology in another universe that popped into being through the back side of a black hole in an entirely different dimension.

Ok, I've gone overboard in those uncharted waters. But try this: a single memory is to the individual brain as an individual is to his community. That is to say that an individual and his community can be modeled as a pattern of interferences, just another level of complexity. So when you change the way an individual thinks of himself, you change the way he lives in his community and thereby you change the community in some way, maybe more, maybe less, that is not predictable. (I'll talk about Chaos in the next chapter.) Colquitt, Georgia, home of the Swamp Gravy project, is an example of this sort of cascade.*

In the holographic model, our world is held–"enfolded" is the favored physics word–in time and space (and however many more dimensions there are), and these dimensions are enfolded into one another like the colors twisted together in some very large all-day sucker. Or, another way to suggest the holographic model: time and space and all the other dimensions we do not yet understand are caught in interference patterns or some other kind of energetic order, what is being called "oscillating possibilities."

We cannot ever literally see these patterns. Seeing with our eyes is limited anyway. Humans are only capable of seeing the unfolded, secondary manifestations of things, not their source. We don't get the whole picture. We see "the map, not the territory," to rephrase Alfred Korzybski. First, we do not register all the things we do see; we habitually practice an inattentional blindness.** Second, we see what we expect to see and not necessarily what is there even when we do try to look. Third, we literally do not see things *in* the world; we "see" images created in our brains. So, we construct a version of reality (what our culture says is reality, those pesky memes again) from frequencies that transcend time and space, and more, are affected by our attention. Light is a particle or a wave depending literally on how you look at it. All this supports the Buddhist teaching which says that the world as we know it is an illusion. Plato's Allegory of the Cave gets a second look. How'd he know that?

So, the question becomes, "How can I open my eyes?" Or maybe, "What can I open besides just my eyes?"

The jewel, at the end of all this, is that if the energy is changed in one human being around one single event, the interference pattern changes (however minutely) through the whole of time (because time is not linear) and space because everything, through the zero point field, is connected.

◃ THE ASTERISKS ▹

*When I first went to Colquitt, Georgia, most of the shops on the square were vacant and boarded up. The square was essentially dead except for pigeons in the lofts of buildings. The last time I was there (eight years after I first went to Colquitt), nothing on the square was vacant, there were small businesses all the way around. Now, I'm an artist, and I know from experience art does not create wealth. The art we created did not make the money to open shops on the square again. The art we made did change people's perceptions of their place, and that changed the square. Make no mistake, the change in perception was aided/driven by some very smart people, and there is no question it took some money to do it, but Colquitt became, to the residents, a place that was worth keeping and investing in, and that showed in the revived economy of the square.

But there is more now. Note that social programs keep people; building renovations help keep place.

1. Project Bounce is an after-school program for disadvantaged kids and adults.

2. The New Life Learning Center is a place for children and adults to participate in art. There is a kiln, paints, clay, paper, old tin roof waiting to be turned into whatever someone wants to try. Art everywhere.

3. A continuing education program is especially important for those who quit school because of poverty or pregnancy or both.

4. The Workforce Investment Agency (WIA) is a service like the continuing-education program, but along with education, the WIA finds jobs for those in the program.

5. A museum.

6. The Market on the Square: a shop on the square—one of those previously boarded-up storefronts—with low rent for local artists and farmers to offer their wares for sale to the public.

7. A fully renovated cotton warehouse, turned theater. The town found a way to reconfigure an old cotton warehouse. Instead of getting rid of it, they found a new use for it.

8. Ten murals now grace the walls of the town. Colquitt is the first designated Mural Town in the state of Georgia, placing it on national and international registers for tourism. All of the murals are based on stories from the community, past and present, and they represent the people there: Native Americans, field workers, black and white, the black community, and the white community. There are pictures of people at work, play, and life there.

9. The Tarrer Inn Bed and Breakfast Hotel (on the Square) is a really nice place to stay. There are real antiques in the rooms and good food (the next decent motel is twenty miles away). The Tarrer is sometimes used as a conference center, and Swamp Gravy people are teaching other people how to do this.

⊰⊱

**The argument for the value of inattentional blindness is that selective perception is a defense against too much input. Temple Grandin, an autistic woman, is most articulate on the subject of too much vision. One of the problems associated with autism is too much input, and Grandin gives you a sense of the problem.

I can speak about another sense. I have a seventy-percent hearing loss in both ears, as measured in an audiologist's sound-proof room where hearing capacity is tested with a series of sounds and spoken words in a variety of volumes and ranges. I am the proud owner of a good hearing aid which improves my percentages somewhat in that soundproof room. It is a digital hearing aid, so it has a program that can reduce background noise. I don't use the aid as I'm supposed to. I find wearing it truly exhausting, even with its squelch program turned on, because my brain no longer has the auditory inattentional capacity of a nor-mal-hearing person. It doesn't edit from consciousness what I don't need. It pays as much attention to a vacuum cleaner as it does to a human voice. I do wear the hearing aid. I use it when I need to be social and it is a useful tool. But even with it, I still have to see a person's lips in order to understand them (which is exactly what I have to do without the hearing aid), and that is because there is so very much extraneous noise even with the hearing aid's squelch turned on. We live, according to me who can't hear very well, in a brutally noisy culture. So I have an understanding of, and respect for, an inattentional capacity.

In the meantime, working with peoples' stories, I spend some time trying very hard to hear what other people say. Previously, in another of The Asterisks sections, I wrote about "rage at being left out." I'd name my hearing as the root source of a lot of that anger. Hearing loss is isolating. I suspect most people who have lost substantial amounts of their hearing over the course of their lives hold some anger about "being left out" whether they want to or not.

To make sense of people's speech, I have to pay very close attention. I get conversation from context and lip reading. But speech is not the only way we talk to one another. Once you start paying even a little extra attention, there is more to know besides what comes in words. I really do see (now) like nobody else I know sees. I consistently catch things visually that others miss.

So the brain plays with capacity—mine, by letting in more visual information as I learn to use it.

This from the fraternal neurolinguistic programming resource: an ordinary person's consciousness is capable of holding seven (five to nine, the average is seven) pieces of information at any given time and that's it. (This is, supposedly, why local phone numbers are seven digits long.) The information is a stream, and in a variety of modes (visual, auditory, tactile), but seven is the magic number. So an inattentional capacity keeps the conscious mind from being overwhelmed. And a shortage of input from one source will be taken up by another. (Meditation can be thought of as focusing this stream onto one single thing.) An overload from one source will eclipse another. Example: I'm a wretched driver with my hearing aid turned on in my ear. I can't pay as much attention to what I'm seeing and vision is my most dependable source of information. I don't have the attention to pay, my seven slots are otherwise occupied with overwhelming vehicle and traffic noise that everybody else just tunes out.

Try an inattentional experiment: wear earplugs and notice how vision intensifies. Even just a few hours will give a sense of the change. For a person who hears normally, a blindfold will do the same thing for auditory capacity.

There is a sort of Aesop's Fable for me in all this, that isn't from Aesop and isn't a fable, but I think of it like Aesop probably intended the fables to be used. Claudius, a three-legged dog of my acquaintance, is missing one of his forelegs. It was amputated at the shoulder courtesy of a Florida alligator. I kept the dog one summer as a favor to his owner. Claudius is one of those dogs who, when days turn hot, likes to keep cool by laying his belly in a hole in the ground. Not just any old hole will do. Has to be a fresh hole. Good-sized, too, because Claudius is a good-sized dog. Given the physics of heat transfer, he requires a new hole every couple of hours. So he digs them. He oughtn't to be able to do it, what with one leg having to do double duty (standing and digging), but no one has ever made him understand this, so he digs a new hole whenever the need arises.

Watching that dog turn my grassy yard into a field of holes that summer reframed my understanding of "disability." Claudius, the three-legged can-do hole-digger, is a far more useful model for me than anything the audiologist (and by extension, my culture, and if I'm not careful, my own thinking and feeling) says to me about the failure of my ears to process sound waves in the usual manner. "Seventy-percent loss is really severe, Ms. Carson, how do you manage your life?" I think of that dog, his impossible holes, his extravagant pleasure in them, and I pay attention the best way I know how.

Further Practice

ABOUT THE HOLOGRAPHIC MODEL OF THE UNIVERSE (AND MORE)

Pribram, M.D., Karl. "The Holographic Brain," DVD. Berkeley, CA: Thinking Allowed Productions.

This documentary was part of a national PBS series. You can find it at: www.thinkingallowed.com.

Talbot, Michael. *The Holographic Universe.* New York: HarperCollins Publishers, 1991.

This book covers the basics on the holographic model of the universe, and discusses who is thinking that way and why.

_____. *Mysticism and the New Physics.* London: Arkana, 1993.

This book makes similar parallels to the points I'm trying to make. You study this stuff and you can't help but see it.

Wilber, Ken, editor. *The Holographic Paradigm and Other Paradoxes: Exploring the Leading Edge of Science.* Boston: Shambhala Publications, 1982.

This is a Pribram reference. The book is a series of compare/contrast conversations involving a brain specialist (Pribram), a quantum physicist and a religious mystic.

ABOUT PERCEPTION

Gladwell, Malcolm. *Blink: The Power of Thinking Without Thinking.* New York: Back Bay Books, 2007.

Blink is a must-read perception book. I listed it before in regards to Paul Ekman's work. Gladwell is also the author of *The Tipping Point: How Little Things Make a Big Difference*, which is about how things catch on, become fashionable, or become social "epidemics." It is relevant to the thinking about Chaos Theory and memes.

Grandin, Temple and Catherine Johnson. *Animals in Translation: Using the Mysteries of Autism to Decode Animal Behavior.* Orlando, FL: Harcourt, 2006.

Grandin is autistic and experiences life outside what we think of as normal perception. She speaks for herself here. She doesn't like Rupert Sheldrake's ideas, but I do. Oliver Sacks wrote about her in *Anthropologist on Mars*.

THREE NODS TO THE GODDESS
TIAMAT/MAMA CHAOS

WHILE WE'RE STILL OSCILLATING with all those time and space possibilities, another relevant idea comes from Chaos Theory: "sensitive dependence of initial conditions." This means that tiny differences in the input of an energetic system can become huge differences in the output of that system. Said another way: little changes can create big results. This is well-known stuff. It applies to how Earth's weather works, and it is a description of turbulence in water and in air. An example used by Chaos theorists is that a butterfly fluttering its wings in China can set in motion forces that become a hurricane in Texas. (Didn't Confucius say something similar? A butterfly flaps its wings and rain falls in Shanghai . . . How'd he know that in 500 B.C.?) What is also true is that the butterfly fluttering its wings can also set in motion forces that create fine weather in Shanghai and Texas, and snow flurries in the Himalayas. If I change the energy around a story, I am potentially a sort of Chaos butterfly. I have that potential because everything is energy, and it is all connected (say quantum physics and all the energy traditions). I don't think I've made any hurricanes in Texas (maybe a few Himalayan snow flurries), but the story work has made many, many small changes in communities over the course of the thirty projects for which I've written plays.

147

Another possibility within the concept of "sensitive dependence" is for altering the patterns of a different energy system, a personal one. Energy-healing traditions say "like attracts like" in this ki energy. If I can learn to live in love and joy, I will attract that energy to me and create that in the energy around me. This is very close to the teaching of Christ, sans the overlay put on it by two thousand years of organized religion. It is also straight Buddhist teaching. I create good energy in my being by how I feel about things that happen to and around me. Emotion has more power in energy matters than does rational thought. If I am angry, I will attract events (energy) that make me more angry. I call to me more and more of whatever emotion I already hold. What I feel is what I get. So when I change the feeling around a story, Chaos says I am making a small change to the input of a system which has the potential to make a large change in the outcome. I am potentially changing the balance of what individuals attract to themselves. Then the individuals make their own input in a similarly sensitive system, their community, and so on . . .

Not every flight of a butterfly makes a hurricane; not every re-visioning of a story has a noticeable impact on an individual or a community, but Chaos says the impact is there whether I notice it or not. Chaos also says the potential is there, the mechanics are in place, for really big changes from the very smallest of inputs.

The second nod to Chaos concerns fractals. A fractal is a kind of pattern made by a chaotic system. A fractal is a comparable but not identical pattern, repeating at different levels of complexity. For instance, if you know trees, you can tell what kind of tree you are seeing even during the winter when it does not have leaves. A walnut tree has a different pattern of bark and limbs from an oak or from anything else. No two walnut trees are exactly the same but the walnut pattern is always recognizable. There are a couple of levels of fractal complexity in the tree example: the first is basic *tree* (roots, trunk, bark, branches, needles or leaves, etc.) as opposed to, say, *shrub* or *vine*. The second level is the specific kind of tree, a walnut tree instead of an oak. Both are identifiable by their pattern, first as trees, then identifiable again in the detail the pattern gives about the specific kind of tree.

Stories can be thought of as another kind of fractal, all similar but with tremendous variety. Stories take their patterns from the decisions and actions people take in the events the stories recount. When I am working with other people's stories, reading the oral histories I'm given, I look for points of decision. Without a decision, I do not have a story. I may have a lovely (or awful) description of something. I may have a joke or anecdote of some kind. I may have the wanderings of a wondrously deranged mind. I may even have something I can use—but I will have to add a decision somewhere in it to make it work as a story onstage. The single thing, the pattern that separates a story from anything else, is a decision on the part of a person somewhere in the story.

Fractal geometry (much of which became visible with computer modeling) shows that the addition of energy into a system will often cause that system to rearrange itself. And often, it rearranges itself around what is called an attractor or a strange attractor. Think of the eye of a hurricane as a strange attractor. A decision in a story is also an attractor. A decision organizes a story out of events in the same way that a higher level of energy in a system can organize a strange attractor. When I create a passage past a dragon, what I am doing most often is clarifying a decision, and thereby giving events a strange (and sometimes, if I'm lucky, wondrous) attractor.*

The third nod to Chaos Theory is quick and huge: without the input of energy into systems, without change, the second law of thermodynamics (good ole Isaac Newton) is one hundred percent accurate and entropy is the result. This is true in traditionally understood energy systems, it is also true in human energy systems. Change or die is the bottom line. Just don't ask a Trickster to make your changes for you.**

⊰ THE ASTERISKS ⊱

*Here are a couple of short pieces, both stories in which I played with a "decision" in the passage past the dragon to make them work for the stage. Both are from the Mennonite community in Newport News, Virginia.

A MAN: I was coming back from fishing that day, I'd been working on the river about five years and I felt like I knew my way around. I did. But that day, there was the worst fog I'd ever been in. I couldn't see shore. I couldn't see more than about ten feet in front of me. I was headed home, steering by compass. Except it felt wrong, it just felt really wrong. Felt like I was going the opposite direction to what I should have been going. I have a pretty good sense of direction, always worked before, and I began to doubt the compass. How do you doubt a compass? Maybe I'd done something that changed the magnetism somehow, I couldn't imagine what, but I'd been out for a while and I'd done a lot on that trip. Or maybe the polarity of the world had changed, it does sometimes. Not very often, once every blue million years, but it does change. Or maybe the compass was just messed up somehow. All I knew for sure was that the direction I was going felt really wrong. So I turned around. And I went a very long way before I found anything I knew. The compass was right. It was way into the night by the time I got home, but the fog had lifted by then and, even in the dark, I could see my way home.

The compass story in the oral history was rambling, and I don't know for sure that the man ever really "turned around." I do know he was lost for a long time in fog, and he genuinely doubted his compass in the process. In the writing, I gave the story the doubt and then, a decision.

A WOMAN: There were several children—my brothers and sisters—at our house growing up and my parents set out to make each one of us, in some way, special. My oldest sister was "our best student," my oldest brother was "going to be as handsome as his father," my other brother was "the best help we have around here," my other sister was "our creative one." And then, there was me: "and this is our pancake eater!" The pancake eater. And with the name always came another pancake. I ate every single one of the extra pancakes. I ate them because I wanted to be something, and pancake eater seemed to be the only thing available. I knew the pancake eater wouldn't starve, they'd have to keep feeding me pancakes to make sure I was still the eater of them. I felt pancake eater was a position of some security, more security than any of my brothers or sisters had, but somehow with less honor in it. I wondered if every family had to have a pancake eater, if it was somehow necessary like mother, father, and the eater of pancakes. But I never met another, nobody else ever owned up to being one. I'll say this: I don't cook pancakes now. I lost my taste for them years ago.

In the oral history, the woman spoke (in about three sentences) of being her family's pancake eater when she was a child and said that she wasn't really pleased with the title but there wasn't anything to do about it, so she ate the pancakes. She made the decision to eat pancakes, and said so. I just elaborated. I focused the story on the decision. The passage past the dragon is why it was important to that child to eat those extra pancakes even when she didn't want them. And then the clincher is another decision, an adult one—she's lost her taste for pancakes so she doesn't make them now. This is a funny piece onstage.

⚔ ⚔

**Trickster: There are excellent books about Trickster and Trickster's doings, and I don't need to cover the same territory, but I do want to note that every Trickster ever written about or spoken of (Tricksters usually come from oral traditions) is a description of Chaos. If you never thought of Coyote (or Spider or Raven or Loki or Legba or Kokopelli) as the flutter of a butterfly's wing, do it now. Tricksters always show up in a situation or social order that is in stasis or headed that way and Tricksters always disrupt it, usually from some hunger of their own. A Trickster's hunger is always a human or animal hunger, never a divine one, and the change a Trickster brings about is always "imperfect" in that things no longer work like they did before. A Trickster's action is the addition of energy to a system, which causes the system to reorganize itself so that the world is not the same anymore. Tricksters' acts are the literary version of "sensitive dependence of initial conditions."

Further Practice

ABOUT CHAOS

Briggs, John. *Fractals—The Patterns of Chaos: Discovering a New Aesthetic of Art, Science, and Nature.* New York: Simon & Schuster, 1992.

Great pictures in this book.

Gleick, James. *Chaos: Making a New Science.* New York: Penguin, 1987.

This is the science.

Walter, Ph.D., Katya. *Tao of Chaos: Merging East and West.* Austin, TX: Kairos Center, 1994.

This is science, too, but it is also an application of the learning from Chaos to our lives.

ABOUT TRICKSTER

Erodes, Richard and Alfonso Ortiz. *American Indian Trickster Tales.* New York: Viking, 1998.

This book includes a couple of stories about Spider's doings, just in case you want to know.

Hyde, Lewis. *Trickster Makes This World: Mischief, Myth and Art.* New York: Farrar, Straus & Giroux. 1998.

This book is about the Trickster tradition in human thought, and much, much more. If you've an interest in Trickster, read this book. I've read and reread this one; I get more with every reading.

Intent! Intent! and "Praying Rain"

Aᴄᴄᴏʀᴅɪɴɢ ᴛᴏ *The American Heritage Dictionary*, "intent" is "having the mind fastened on some purpose." I prefer the meaning of the Latin root: *intendere*, which means "to stretch toward something." I will use "intent" here to mean a mental stretching toward something, being open to it and expecting it at the same time but without a willful demand. "Intent" is very close in some ways to the concept of "imagining" discussed in the chapter "The Work of Imagination in the Body and in the Energy Around the Body," but "imagining," as I am using it, is about events in the individual's being, whereas "intent" is practiced out in the world.

Intent is a very large idea in both the energy-healing and in the quantum communities. Intent can change things. What things? Energy-healing practitioners say it is those things we stretch toward that can change. What does that mean? Our intent can change what we experience. We experience what we intend. Want to live in joy? There are "how-to-intend-it" instructions that get you that very thing. Or that's the theory. Practice is always harder than theory. You still have to pay the electric bill while you practice.

Quantum physicists are having some wondrous difficulty with intent; much of that little bitty stuff (subatomic particles) is

155

proving richly problematic. Many physicists say that observing an experiment at the subatomic level can alter the subatomic characteristics, and that expecting something specific at the subatomic level can make a difference in the outcome of an experiment. Light behaves like a particle or a wave depending on which kind of experiment you set up. This is a dynamic process if ever there was one. It seems that all of matter can be either a particle or an energetic potential that is not a particle, and it becomes very hard to know what you are seeing, much less to try to explain it. An experimenter's intent makes a difference at the level of quantum physics.

Intent operates at other levels, too. Focused intent toward water can change the pH of the water, change the electrical conductivity of the water, change the shape water crystallizes into, and more. Finding out about the changes in water which can be produced by nothing more than your intent may lead to you standing in your kitchen with a glass of water you plan to drink in your hands *intendere*-ing over it. The more we learn about quantum science, the more intent does seem to matter.

Quantum science says that we find things in our world solid because it is our intent (or something's intent) and our perception that they be solid. Things are certainly not solid by the matter contained in them.* A further edge to this science says there is no reality out there independent of someone (or something) experiencing it.

The energy-healing community also speaks about the energy of intent. Intent is not will. Will is the mental faculty by which one deliberately chooses or decides upon a course of action. "I will practice Reiki." That statement may be true, but it does not make the energy flow in my hands, no matter how many times I stomp my delicate foot and demand it. But this statement can make the energy move: "I intend energy to flow now." I must reach for it, expect it to happen. I imagine the flow of energy like a warm current or like a wash of the love (note that love is an emotion) through my body and out my hands. That's the best description I know of what it feels like. And it begins as I sit here at the computer keyboard. To write about the process of intending energy to flow, I go through feeling it to be able to describe it, and it works.

The discipline of Reiki employs a series of symbols. You learn them as you progress through higher levels of the practice. You are taught that the use of a specific symbol increases the amount of energy flowing through your hands, that another symbol affects long-distance healing, that another is for emotional healing, etc. If I understand the intended meaning of the symbol and its traditional use, and I call that use in appropriate circumstances, I am operating with intent, and intent has energy. I do not want to try to will the symbol to work. All I have to do for the symbol to work like it is supposed to is to see the symbol in my mind (or draw it in the air) and be open to the possibility it offers. The teaching is that the symbols themselves have power (against all rational thinking) and they should have power because they have many years of practitioners' intent behind them.

If I presume to try to "heal" something specific on me or anyone else, if I'm trying to *fix* something, that is an act of will on my part and my hands stay as cool as they were when I started. If I can intend to be about joy, if I can give with no expectation of return, energy flows. (This was hard for me at first, thanks to memes again: in this case, "You are a fool if you don't get a return from your investment!") If I can give with the intent of love and joy, my body and my hands work like a transformer, and my hands get noticeably warmer. It is another dynamic process. The ki has its own astonishing wisdom (Sufi tradition says love is an energy with its own consciousness!) and I get plenty of return, enfolded, ten-folded. This process of intending is not just applicable to practicing Reiki. I used the Reiki example because it is a feel-able example and I can describe it.

The energy-healing traditions go a step further. There is a dual nature to the process they describe. Intent, say the healers, has energy, and the ki itself has intent.

So what can intent change? There are some specifics to talk about. There is a whole genre of self-help these days based on the premise "change your mind, change your life." This has to do with intent even when it is not called by that name in the titles of the books. There is plenty of instruction out there with "intent" in the title, too. My shaman friend runs what he calls "life-scripting" workshops with the same idea. You consciously intend to let go of the things you don't want in your life; consciously intend to draw to you those things you do want. (Be careful what you ask for, you may get it.) A story my friend tells (remember, he's something of a comedian) is that he asked for "more green energy," meaning money but he didn't say *that* (the language around money is its own comedy in the energy-healing community). Two days later, he got an offer he could refuse, to sell an "energy enhancer" made of blue-green algae to his clients as a side endeavor. What he says of that event is that it was intent at work. He just wasn't specific enough about what he intended. Talk to anyone skilled in any of the martial arts. At the higher levels of skill, they are all (sometimes literally) stunningly rich in the practice of intent.

Don Juan's instruction to Castaneda was, from the outset, a training in intent and the gathering of sufficient personal energy to use it. The first thing he taught Castaneda was how to shut up monkey mind, though he did not call it by that name. That is the first step in all the traditions that use intent.

If you are not yet a believer, read the medical studies on the power of prayer. It seems that generalized prayer–like praying for all children or a group of children in general–doesn't seem to make much difference. Directed prayer, saying a prayer for a specific friend's healing, even somebody you don't know (but the prayer is still directed) can make a difference. A prayer to cure cancer specifically does not seem to be as effective as a prayer for the well-being of the person being prayed for. Distance doesn't matter. The number of people praying does seem to make a difference. ("Where three or more are gathered together . . .") Someone who has some understanding or familiarity or comfort with the idea of prayer as intent or as directing energy is likely to make even more of a difference. This is actually measured stuff. There is quantified evidence of the value of prayer/energy healing in people's survival of illness. One example: Elizabeth Targ, M.D., a psychiatrist and a doubter, conducted a series of double-blind experiments in San Francisco with AIDS patients and energy healers, some of whom used prayer as their healing practice. This was before the life-saving chemical cocktail now used for AIDS was developed. Almost all of her subjects, who unknowingly received focused energy healing, experienced improvement in their condition. Dr. Targ used a variety of healers (forty of them) who worked under several different traditions (some were Native American shamans, some were people who believe in the power of prayer, some were Reiki-like healers, and others) all of whom used intent in some way even if not by that name. She used an entire garden of healers, all of whom could point to some success as healers in the past, and all of whom could work from a distance. She was so astounded after the first experiment that she figured she had to have made some mistake, so she did the experiment again with even more stringent controls. She got the same result. Intent can influence a dynamic system, and our bodies are dynamic systems.

There is a story in Gregg Braden's book *The Isaiah Effect* about the power of prayer in another dynamic system—the weather. If you want the full story from the writer instead of my abbreviated account, read his book. For me it is instruction about the use of intent. Braden was hiking in the southwestern U.S. desert with a Native American rainmaker. There had been an endless siege of drought and the man was going to his medicine wheel to pray for rain. Braden was along because he was interested. He was allowed to go along because he was a friend. The rainmaker came to his medicine wheel, made the proper approach to a sacred endeavor and stood in the center of the wheel speaking in his people's language.

When he finished, Braden asked, "You prayed for rain?"

"No, I prayed rain."

"What do you mean?"

"You pray for rain, you don't get anything. You have to feel the rain, and smell it, see what it does for the land. You have to be in the rain. You have to pray rain. You pray for rain, it doesn't work. You have to pray rain."

And, says Braden, it rained, gully washers, it rained gully washers.

"Yeah," said the rainmaker, "that's the problem, how to turn it off . . ."

Here's the process: you intend the experience you want of the world, you conjure it—and I'm not suggesting some hocus-pocus, I'm calling up the older meanings of the word conjure. You evoke what you want and you feel what it is. In the story above, to "pray for rain" means a person would be praying *from* a condition they *feel* as drought (the need of rain), and it is the feeling they have that carries energy. To pray rain, you must imagine feeling the rain.

Now, have I or anybody I know ever accomplished changes in weather using this technique? Brace yourself, my answer is that maybe I have. I do experiment with this. The day it may have happened was cold and overcast. I was at the horse field and I'd been out a while so I was cold. I was also alone. Using intent is easier for me when I am alone because being in the presence of someone who thinks I'm being foolish is a real distraction. I would not be trying any of it (I wouldn't know that I could try) if I hadn't had the learning that came with Reiki. I *know* that intent works to run energy through my hands so I try using intent in other ways. This cold day, I stood still in an open field and said aloud, "I need some sun." I stood for a minute, maybe a little more, imagining what sun would feel like on my head and shoulders and my back, imagining warmth and light. The sun broke through the clouds. I watched my shadow come into being on the ground and I felt warmth where I'd imagined feeling it. This didn't last long, the clouds closed again, but I had gotten exactly what I intended. Coincidence? Fine, let it be coincidence, but call it significant coincidence, a synchronicity.** And understand the possibility in this: I was applying energy (my intent) to a dynamic system, weather, and Chaos says change of some sort is not just likely to happen, Chaos says some change will happen.

I think about all this when I put people onstage to tell a story that has real meaning to them in a place where that story also has meaning. There is a way in which I am/we are praying rain. Acting, especially in the community situations, has the energy of intent and because intent has the energy it does, I/we had best think about what we are praying. Does this mean I should be writing the equivalent of community sitcoms because they are funny and nobody really suffers anything except a little angst? No. Until we agree somehow to learn from something besides suffering, it is the human condition to suffer. Buddhists, Christians ("It is easier for a rope—new translation—to pass through the eye of a needle than for a rich man to enter heaven . . ."), Toltec, all the energy traditions I know anything about, tell us it is attachment to one thing or another that makes us suffer. It is never that suffering is fun or easy, but it is suffering with no learning and no meaning in it that is hell.

If I must examine suffering (Shall I name St. Cyril's dragon "Sufferin'," shall I name each of his claws by the things we attach to?), then my job when I write a passage past the ole Sufferin' dragon, or when I reframe a story, is to find grace and grace is whatever allows us to truly learn from and let go of the things that hurt.

Buddhist teaching says that great suffering is the surest path to enlightenment. They say it takes suffering to make us *want* constructive change in our lives. Without it, we are too contented and we should honor that ole Sufferin' dragon when we do have to pass him. How's that for a reframe job? ***

Now, like a piece of music that instructs the musician to repeat, go back and reread this book and for "old pain" or "hard stories" read "old attachments."

We get what we feel. We call it to us. If we change what we feel, we can change what we get. If you intend to learn to use intent, speak your intent out loud. Just thinking a little about something sometimes is not being invested in the intent business. Talk out loud and mean it. Do not ever try to call bad stuff to somebody else, it comes straight to you, it is your intent calling it. Don't use negatives when you speak with intent. Speak in the present tense. The subconscious doesn't get negatives and time is always now. The subconscious is involved in intent. Huna says it is the "lower self" that does most of the energetic talking. "I don't want to be miserable anymore" reads in the subconscious as, "I do want to be miserable." "I'm healthy!" or "I am happy!" is a far better statement for using intent. Intent works for abstract things.

("Abstract" is don Juan's naming; you can also say it works for energetic things.) So it can be a way to increase your well-being, including your economics, but it is not the way to get a million dollars in the mail. Intent is never ever about just wishing for something. Intent is out loud and active and it is a genuine way to affect those things subject to chaos, which includes your body and your well-being.

◄ THE ASTERISKS ►

*The atom. This is an image from Bill Bryson's book *A Short History of Nearly Everything*. He is referring to William H. Crooper, speaking about size relationships in an atom of matter, and I'm paraphrasing. Take a single atom, say, a carbon atom—one of the most common on this Earth—and blow it up to the size of Notre Dame Cathedral in Paris. Its nucleus (that's the neutrons and protons in the middle) will be about the size of a house fly and the electrons will be running around the outer edges of the cathedral. The fly-sized nucleus will weigh more than the cathedral does. The electrons, invisible even at this scale, seem to be there sometimes and at other times not. Where do they go? Good question.

Say this to a high school student, and he's likely to say, "Yeah, yeah, I know, a little green pea in a football field . . ."

That's what matter is made of. That's what matters in matter. Well, it is not all that matters, evidently, but if all that space is what matter is made of, why can I not put my hand through the computer keyboard? Well, because the space isn't exactly empty. Seems that nothing is empty, not even the vast space in the universe. Not empty at all. Not even the least little bit empty. It's just not got the realized particles of matter in it. Ok, so what is there? Energy, patterns of energy, "oscillating possibilities." What are "oscillating possibilities"? Well, you got me. And you got most everybody else, too. Nobody can tell you exactly what "oscillating possibilities" are, except maybe you can say that they are unrealized matter (current thinking). But what does that mean? Nothing is empty, not even the space in the universe.

"The universe is not just queerer than we think, it is queerer than we can imagine." Sir James Jeans, a mathematician, seems to have said it first (I've seen different attributions for the quote), but I suspect lots of folks have said it again and again and again since. Probably gets said daily, if not by the hour, out at the edge of quantum physics.

⊰ ⊱

** Another of my lessons in the energy of intent came after I read Rupert Sheldrake's *Dogs That Know When Their Owners Are Coming Home and Other Unexplained Powers of Animals.* The book documents an experiment in which Sheldrake tested pets (mostly dogs but not exclusively) who seemed to know when their owners were coming home. He set up a video camera with a clock in it, focused on the place where the dog usually waited for its owner's arrival. To remove the chance of habit, the owners left work at odd times of the day and they'd drive a different car so it wouldn't be the sound of a car engine the dog recognized. The dogs consistently did not move into their waiting position until the owner's thoughts really turned toward going home. When the owner's thoughts did turn toward home, however late or early from the normal, the dogs did go to their waiting positions. No special effort was made on the part of the owners to think, I'm going home now, just the real doing (the intent) of going home. In fact, thinking about going home without the intention of really doing it did not bring the dogs to their waiting positions. The dogs were evidently sensitive to their absent owners' real intentions.

I started paying attention to my dog after I read the book and got a similar result. I travel occasionally for work and when I leave home, I usually don't know exactly how long I will be gone, so my house-sitter doesn't know when I'm coming home either. Bear Dog has a hard time when I am gone. She knows the difference between when I pack a suitcase and when I don't, so none of this applies to my trips to the grocery store or just around town. When I leave with a suitcase, she is bereft. She lies on my bed–I give over the bed for the duration, there isn't any choice, I might as well be gracious about it–and she doesn't want to eat or go outside. Boarding her is worse. (Taking in a second dog so Bear didn't lose her whole pack in my absence was a nightmare.) If I leave home with a suitcase, the sitter has to put a leash on the dog and oblige her to move. My regular house-sitter can tell when I start home, he recognizes the change in the dog's behavior. She takes an interest in what's going on again, she wants her food in a timely fashion and goes about her things of dog life in our household until fifteen or twenty minutes before I pull into the driveway. Then she watches for me out the front door. Sheldrake's right (in my less than scientific experiment). My intent to come home seems to be communicated somehow over distance to my dog.

The second dog story is a very different take on intent. The second dog I took in, Zelda, had serious aggression problems by the time she was four. I had been bitten badly rescuing a neighbor's dog from her killing bite. Her killing bite: take something live by the back of its neck, bite it really hard, pick it up and shake it until its neck broke and it died. This was her favorite trick. She went through a lot of opossums. I was bitten by a dog she was about to kill (I did manage to save it), and that wasn't the first dog fight I had to break up. My brother looked at my ripped hand, me with my head between my legs to keep from fainting, and said, "Let me give you a piece of advice for the next time you decide to get in a dog fight. To win any fight, you have to enter the fight with more energy than the fighters, and to stop a dog fight, you have to enter the fight with more energy than the dogs, and if they are trying to kill each other, you better be really serious or you're going to get really hurt." I broke up one more dog fight. Zelda attacked Bear, and by the time I got there, blood was flying. Zelda couldn't do her standard kill trick (Bear, at the time, was a sixty-pound dog and Zelda was about fifty pounds), but Bear was fighting for her life and losing. "Find more energy than the dogs." Whoa. Except, I looked at the situation calmly. I picked up a heavy dinner plate, with the leavings of a meal still on it, and I broke the plate over Zelda's head and knocked her out. It didn't take great strength, it didn't take much risk on my part and I didn't get hurt at all. I learned the value of a bigger stick? A bigger stick is useful, no question, but application of that moment's bigger stick, the dinner plate, was due to the energy of intent. The wisdom of breaking a dinner plate over the attacking dog's head is obvious, but the moment of doing it, the easy calculated ferocity of that act was a surprise to me.

My horse, Kate (the diva who chews the scenery), has been a third kind of education in intent. Seventeen years of Kate's lessons can be summed up very easily: if I'm willful, she's willful (and she's half a ton bigger than I am). If I can hold intent lightly, playfully, if I can keep my mind and body focused on what we are together, she returns the favor and the trust. My focus cannot be about what we have just done. It cannot be about what we have done wrong, it cannot even be about what we have just done right. It is never about anything in the past, not even the momentary past, but it is not about the future either. Focus is about now and I have to "intend" focus to hold it. Meditation is a similar endeavor. A musician "in the groove" is in the same place. An athlete performing at the top of his game is in the same place. When I can do this with my horse, it allows me to ride right. Kate lives in an ever-moving now. When I can intend that "now place" in my own being, it makes for those times in which the horse and I are a third creature together, something different than the sum of our parts. There are some obvious qualifiers: first, there are some skills a rider has to learn because without those skills, you spend too much time worrying about what you just did wrong and that makes for very hard bouncing, mostly on the saddle, but sometimes on the ground. Second, horses are made for forward motion. You can almost say they are made *of* forward motion—the inclination to flight in the face of perceived danger is one of the stronger instincts a horse has, and I have to honor that. I cannot ask for something that is against my partner's being. But when I can *intend* our forward motion with my body and mind together, she gets it and she seems to take as much pleasure in those times as I do. Are we perfect? We are not. This is hard for me to do, the past is a familiar intrusion on my consciousness, and I've been working toward learning this for years. She is certainly more willing now to help find those moments than she was when I first bumped along on her back. One way to speak of this is to say we have learned how to play together. Another way: Kate taught her human how to ride a horse. Another way: I have learned to talk *with* my horse in a way that makes sense to her. It is the language of intent.

⊰ ⊱

***Another reframe. There is a story from Islamic tradition in which Satan, the angel, refused to worship God's creation, Adam, as God commanded. He could not worship Adam as commanded because *he loved God too much* to worship someone or something other than God. When he was banished from Heaven for non-compliance, his torment was due to being separated from that which he loved. Sin, in this version of the story, is loving something too much, being too attached, loving obsessively.

In this version of the story, Satan is another "Trickster," a creature whose hunger was so great that it reorganized the world, and "hell" is a situation in which you cannot have that which you love. It is certainly another way to think about what that ole Sufferin' dragon might really be.

Further Practice

ABOUT THE ATOM DESCRIPTION

Bryson, Bill. *A Short History of Nearly Everything.* New York: Broadway Books, 2005.

This is a great history of scientific learning. If it had been an introductory textbook in college, I might have studied physics. Bryson is very, very funny.

ABOUT FOCUSED INTENTION AND WATER

Emoto, Dr. Masauru, translated by David A. Ihayne. *The Hidden Messages in Water.* Hillsboro, OR: Beyond Words Publishing, 2004.

This is mostly pictures. You will be amazed.

Tiller, Ph.D., William; Dibble, Jr., Ph.D., Walter and Michael Kohane, Ph.D. *Conscious Acts of Creation: The Emergence of a New Physics.* Walnut Creek, CA: Pavior Publications, 2001.

This book is hard reading for someone who is not literate in mathematics. I am not literate beyond what I learned in high school algebra. What I did was skip most of the mathematical proof and read how the experiments were done and the outcome of them (they are in English, I can handle English).

ABOUT INTENT

Braden, Gregg. *The Isaiah Effect: Decoding the Lost Science of Prayer and Prophecy.* New York: Harmony Books, 2000.

A how-to-pray book. I find the "praying rain" story truly compelling.

Burnham, Sophy. *The Path of Prayer: Reflections on Prayer and the True Stories of How It Affects Our Lives.* New York: Viking Compass, 2002.

This is a how-to book with soul.

Byrne, Rhonda. *The Secret.* New York: Atria Books, 2006.

This is a how-to book with not much soul. The title of this one might be *How to Get More Money.* What I do like about this book is the contributors, the people who are quoted.

Dossey, M.D., Larry. *Healing Words: The Power of Prayer and the Practice of Medicine.* San Francisco: HarperSanFrancisco, 1993.

In this book there are good examples of successes (and failures) of the power of prayer.

Dyer, Dr. Wayne W. *The Power of Intention: Learning to Co-create Your World.* Carlsbad, CA: Hay House, 2004.

Dyer is a very popular new-age lecturer, and a good teacher. He has published a number of related books, all of which are current-thinking, how-to books in making the most of your mind and body relationships.

Herrigel, Eugen. *Zen in the Art of Archery.* New York: Vintage Books, 1989.

A traditional text on the use of intent.

McTaggart, Lynne. *The Intention Experiment: Using Your Thoughts to Change Your Life and the World.* New York: Free Press, 2007.

This is the second time I've listed this book: truly recommended reading.

Wilson, Robert Anton. *Prometheus Rising.* Tempe, AZ: New Falcon Publications, 1983.

This is a how-to book about using intent. Wilson comes from a neurolinguistic programming perspective; this is something of a foundation book for NLP.

RELEVANT SHELDRAKE

Sheldrake, Ph.D., Rupert. *Dogs That Know When Their Owners Are Coming Home and Other Unexplained Powers of Animals.* New York: Crown Publishing, 1999.

One of the questions Sheldrake asked in his *Seven Experiments* book is whether some dogs really do know this, and he set out to answer the question.

_____. *Seven Experiments That Could Change The World: A Do-It-Yourself Guide to Revolutionary Science.* Rochester, VT: Parkstreet Press, 2002.

This is an interesting series of potential experiments. Sheldrake outlines the current thinking on each of them and discusses possibilities about how they might happen. Sheldrake found himself at difficult odds with the conservative scientific community for his ideas, and set out to prove some of them by truly ingenious rigidly controlled testing.

Time and the Storyteller

Quantum physics (and quantum physics isn't alone

I WENT TO A CONFERENCE right after I'd written that sentence fragment during the first draft of this book. The sentence was a fragment because, while I knew what I was going to try to write about, I didn't have much of an idea how to do it, and I literally didn't know what word might come next. I stopped with that fragment and turned off the computer. This paragraph and the rest of this section were written after the conference.

The conference I went to was the yearly get-together of the supporters of The Light Center at Black Mountain, North Carolina. The Light Center is devoted to teaching effective prayer. The Light Center attracts something a little outside what you might think of as normal prayer-conference attendees. There were healers, psychics and many others who have found the power of prayer to be miraculous. I am a believer in prayer, but it is the "praying rain" variety of prayer and not the stuff that starts with addressing a Heavenly Father and never mentions a Heavenly Mother or a Holy Earth or Blessed Energy or Holy Spirit—Rukha d'Koodsha is her name from Aramaic (pronounced Rooka d'Koosha). It never mentions a Blessed Life or any of the overwhelming multitude of other things that may truly be holy. Prayer as usual usually whines to the H.F. about the sorry state of being here below. I ran from a tradition that told me women were a source of sin. I ran because that and a lot of other things felt just plain wrong. Then I began to read (the story of my life, I read something). I am sure now that much of what I was taught in Baptist Sunday school was just plain wrong. More, I can get into that Jesus guy. He was a long-haired hippie radical who recommended questioning authority (my meme!) and taught letting go of attachments and learning to live in love (agape). After my reading, I could walk into a Christian church again without wanting to do something to ward off hexes and I could go to a prayer conference in Black Mountain in relative good faith.

I was the opening-night speaker at The Light Center conference. I did a piece that includes the spider story (told in the Introduction of this book) and the waking up that came after it. After I had spoken, a woman I didn't know, and certainly didn't know to be a psychic, said, "I like what you just did, but the thing you are working on at home about quantum physics and time and storytelling is more important."

I had written

Time and the Storyteller
Quantum physics (and quantum physics isn't alone

just a few hours before. The computer that held those words was turned off ninety miles away from Black Mountain.

So, with that jolt from the blue (-haired woman), let me start again . . .

Quantum physics (and quantum physics isn't alone, the energy traditions have been teaching the same thing for much longer) says that time is not linear. It is only our perception that makes it seem linear (we see the map, not the territory). Real time is somehow enfolded (remember all the colors wrapped around one another in the all-day sucker) and everything is happening concurrently, just maybe not in the same universe. See, universes may be enfolded too. Or the universes may be enfolded at a series of different levels of resonance. Do I understand this? Not in the way I understand that it took me a certain number of minutes to write this paragraph after I got back to the home (and the dog) I had left two days before.

Did that woman breach time or space or both to know what I was working on? Wrong question. Hold on to the idea of non-linear time as a possibility.

In Castaneda's book *The Power of Silence* there is a page-and-a-half-long passage in which don Juan says that some practitioners of his way of being were storytellers. He asks Castaneda what he would think of a storyteller who changed the facts of a story. The story don Juan uses to illustrate is one from the Yaqui Indians' oral tradition. It is a story of a revolutionary who incited an uprising and was shortly captured, and drawn and quartered, by the Spanish. What if, asks don Juan, in the storyteller's version of this story, the man's uprising was successful? Castaneda answers that he might consider this storyteller a psychotic patriot, someone who wanted his people's salvation so badly that he had deluded himself into making a happier ending to the story. Don Juan says that Castaneda is missing the point. He says that when the storyteller tells the story his way, so that the revolution was successful, and then throws his hat to the ground and turns it three-hundred-and-sixty degrees (full circle, counter-clockwise), then in this universe, or some other, the revolution is successful, the revolutionary's goal has transcended his person and what we think of as history.

Now, do I believe this? It is hard. I'm operating just fine in linear time. I'm warming what really seems to be a cup of coffee that was hot and sat too long and got cold. I'm warming it in a thing called a microwave that really seems to do the job of warming it a second time. But I'm no longer willing to claim I know for sure about that drawn-and-quartered revolutionary. Be amused: the point that hangs me up in don Juan's story is the part about the storyteller throwing his hat on the ground and turning it. It is—in that context—a gesture of intent.

And intent has energy.

There is speculation in the quantum world that not only is energy truly infinite, it is also infinitely creative (and infinite is not nearly a big enough word). In the moment in this universe in which I warm the cup of cold coffee, there is another whole universe in which *my* coffee does not need warming and another in which I am drinking tea and another in which *my* being is incapable of drinking anything because I don't have a mouth and these universes are there—BAM!—simply because I sit here at this computer, in this universe, in this world, in this country, in this chair, and I think of the possibility of them. This energy is not only infinite, it is hugely, enormously, endlessly, astoundingly creative.

Am I feeling large and powerful? Are we having fun making all those new universes?

The next question: Is there a universe or a time enfolded some way in this infinite energy in which the revolutionary in don Juan's story is successful? The storyteller, not to mention the drawn-and-quartered revolutionary, certainly intended it.

And who intended what happened to the story of that other revolutionary, the one we call Jesus? Who, metaphorically speaking, threw a hat (or miter) on the ground and turned it three-hundred-and-sixty degrees that time? It was at the Council of Nicaea (325 A.D.) when the story of that revolutionary got reworked in order to consolidate the power of the Catholic Church. It is a *fact* that the story got changed. New translations of the Dead Sea Scrolls reveal just how radical some of the changes were. More, there is a Gospel of Mary Magdalene. The fragment we have of her book suggests a radically different story, at least about her, than the ones I was taught all those years ago in Sunday school. Christians have been living with the changed story since the Council of Nicaea as though it were a real one. Believers have killed plenty of people in the name of that changed story and it hasn't stopped yet.

So what is real here?

Shamanic traditions say that when the shaman retrieves pieces of his or her client's soul, the client's past is literally changed. I've learned, from the story work I've done, that when hard events come to have a meaning in people's lives other than just pain, the effect of what we think of as the past is changed in a person's body and in the energy around the body, and that can begin a cascade of other changes (remember the holographic model).

This energy I'm trying to speak of, this energy-in-the-moment which allows the woman at the prayer conference to know what I've been working on at home, is a field. It is not an "event" like visible light that races through space. So the blue-haired lady doesn't have to breech time or space. It is all right there in the field. This field is the same stuff that matters in matter. Call the field: Teilhard de Chardin's "noosphere" or Rupert Sheldrake's "morphogenic field." Call it those "oscillating possibilities." Or, call it "zero point field" as quantum physics does.

Some part of this field even seems to have a number at which it can be accessed. Proven psychics experience their insights when their brainwaves are operating at 7.8 cycles per second. One physicist, Dr. Valerie V. Hunt (her book that recounts this experiment is *Infinite Mind: Science of the Human Vibrations of Consciousness*), measured brainwaves of people who claimed psychic ability, and she found that number quite consistent among them. It is where they all "went" in preparation for opening their minds to whatever insights might come. So the woman at Black Mountain adjusted her brainwaves to "the field." We can learn to adjust them consciously. This is meditation again—brainwaves slow down (at first) in meditative states. You can find the levels in your own brain, and learn to recognize them. Someone who has psychic ability has figured out how to access a specific frequency with some consistency, 7.8 cycles per second, and she knows something of what I'm working on. Do I think that woman somehow went to my turned-off computer and looked at it? No. I think she read energy. But how does she choose what to see or know? She doesn't exactly. She can adjust her brain and direct her focus and she did that, she directed it at me. Time and the storyteller was what I'd been thinking about. Beyond that, she just picks up something of what is out there in the "field."

If that "field" is not constrained by time or space, it is going to take something more than our normal twenty-percent brain engagement to say whether the past is or is not changed when someone begins to think differently about an event that happened to them and the energy of that event is changed in their body. The energy-healing traditions say the past is truly changed. I am willing to entertain the possibility of change because in-the-moment effects can be seen so graphically with the story work.

I take the experience at Black Mountain as a gift, another of the synchronicities I love and welcome. The woman gave me an example of the mutability of time and space when she knew what I had been working on, ninety miles away at my literary salt mine in a part of my life that had nothing to do with being the evening's keynote speaker at The Light Center. That mutability was the very thing I was beginning to try to write about back at my salt mine. I had not understood how to approach my subject matter when I turned the computer off. She gave me an example to use in my approach.

The study of synchronicity suggests that "meaningful coincidences" often come at moments of need. Bear #75 did come to my door at a moment of need. I wanted to write a bear, I needed her (Bear #100 in my play) and I was looking for a way to make her work, but I was stuck and I had been for some months. Before the bolt from the blue-haired lady, I was looking for a way to talk about the mutability of time and space. I had written those beginning words as my own gesture of intent but I'd turned off the computer because I didn't know what came next. I often make that gesture when I'm writing—I leave something I can start with when I get back to the work. The words I left hanging were what the blue-haired lady found. Synchronicities also seem sometimes to point the way to move ahead. Both of these did, but both in unexpected ways. And synchronicities seem to arrive by our being open to the possibility of them. Both these situations were open to change, they were dynamic and available to Mama Chaos's tender ministrations.

Enlightenment traditions tell us we could *live* in synchronicity if we could give up what quantum physics tells us is illusion anyway—time and, by extension, all that precious past. Enlightenment traditions also tell us that those endless synchronicities are happening now. We just don't have the perception to see them, thanks (again) to memes and inattention and whatever else is at work. It usually takes a whop-up-the-side-of-the-head-with-that-two-by-metaphor, a knock of the spirit that registers, to persuade us to begin to see.

No past. No past. No past. Ok, but where are Spider and all of us assorted apprentices if there is no past? I don't know. But we are all human, we will still need stories.

Further Practice

ABOUT CHRISTIAN TRADITION

Barnstone, Willis, editor. *The Other Bible*. San Francisco: Harper-SanFrancisco, 1984.

A sourcebook of ancient texts. A reference, not light reading.

Leloup, Jean-Yves (translated from the Coptic and commentaries) and Joseph Rowe (English translation). *The Gospel of Mary Magdalene*. Rochester, VT: Inner Traditions, 2002.

The Gospel itself is fragmentary, but even the fragments are a revolution. Leloup is a theologian.

Mack, Burton L. *The Lost Gospel: The Book of Q and Christian Origins*. San Francisco: HarperSanFrancisco, 1993.

A study of extractions from the New Testament and the Gnostic Gospels of things thought to have come directly from the teachings of Jesus. A radical, question-authority kind of guy, that Jesus . . .

Pagels, Elaine. *Adam, Eve, and the Serpent*. New York: Random House, 1988.

_____. *The Gnostic Gospels*. New York: Vintage Books, 1981.

_____. *The Origin of Satan*. New York: Random House, 1996.

I'd read Pagels if she were writing about stone soup. These are far more interesting.

MORE RECOMMENDED SCIENCE

Greene, Brian. *The Elegant Universe: Superstrings, Hidden Dimensions, and the Quest for the Ultimate Theory.* New York: Vintage Books, 1999.

Greene is writing about what may prove true, this is the further edge of possibility. Fascinating stuff.

Hawking, Ph.D., Stephen. *A Brief History of Time: From the Big Bang to Black Holes.* New York: Bantam Books, 1988.

This is another important book to read if you are striving for an understanding of the quantum business. Nobody promised you this stuff was easy . . .

McTaggart, Lynne. *The Field: The Quest for the Secret Force of the Universe.* New York: HarperCollins, 2002.

The field of the title is the zero point field, and the book is written from conversations with people at that edge of quantum physics. A must-read book.

Smolin, Lee. *The Life of the Cosmos.* New York: Oxford University Press, 1997.

This is wondrous speculation about the origin of the universe backed up by Samolin's discipline and science. What does go on in black holes?

Zukav, Gary. *The Dancing Wu Li Masters: An Overview of the New Physics.* New York: Harper Perennial, 2001.

This is an introduction to quantum physics, and a really good place to start if you want to understand this quantum stuff.

Agency

I'VE BEEN WRITING ABOUT what happens with the big stories I use in making the community plays, the ones that want reframing. Now I want to consider the majority of the stories I use. I make passages past the dragon for almost everything I use, but that is the common work of making plays from people's stories. It is part of the work of making plays from my stories, too. To talk about my concerns with the majority of these stories, I want to introduce an idea that doesn't come from quantum physics or energy work directly but is germane to both: agency.

The American Heritage Dictionary defines agency as: "action, operation, power; the mode or means of action," from the Latin *agentia*: "acting." (Interesting play in the language there . . .) I think of agency as the capacity to act on one's own behalf. Samuel Beckett is one of the few playwrights who ever managed to make drama out of a character's lack of agency (*Waiting for Godot*), most of the rest of us playwrights seem to need it.

There are several aspects of agency I want to explore. The first two are about writing.

One of my jobs in the story work is to give agency to the characters I write. What I mean is that they must be true to themselves. I cannot write a whitewash (or any other kind of wash) of a person's story and be giving agency with what I write. When the real Pen Bascome (the sermon story in the "Neurolinguistic Programmer" chapter on reframing) was murdered those years ago, agency was (obviously) taken from him by the man who shot him. Agency was also taken away from his family and his community when the local newspaper printed the killer's version of those events and that story was accepted as true. That time, it was a whitewash with all the usual implications of the word. I cannot claim that the exchange at the Pearly Gates between Pen Bascome and his killer is true in any sense of being observable or verifiable. What I can claim is that reframing the story, giving Pen Bascome a posthumous opportunity to confront his killer, gave the people who knew the story the opportunity to tell the story they knew as true.

To give agency to characters, I have to somehow be true to both the (emotional/spiritual) experience related in the oral history and the character of the person whose story it is. I often look for a way to deliver an emotional truth and not necessarily a factual one.* I'm trying to make art of life. I cannot write history, it takes too long and it usually isn't very interesting onstage.

What I can do successfully is limited by the depth and breadth of my imagination and skill, but I am willing to try almost anything. Nothing human should be alien—it may be appalling, corrupt, stupid, brutal or wondrous—but it cannot be alien. There are things human beyond my capacity to understand, but that does not mean they are beyond my capacity to try to imagine.

I do make judgments about which stories I'm willing to use and how I use them, choices about what points of view I will or won't make public, and I can be justly accused of choosing in a political way. I try not to use stories that demean others for any of the readily available –isms: race, class, sex, age. I may use a story in which racism is a factor but I try not to give voice to a racist point of view. There are more than plenty other demeaning prejudices in our society that haven't made it to –ism words yet: sexual preference, mental or physical ability, body shape, cultural heritage . . .** There is no shortage. I try to honor an ethic in this work and it comes directly from thinking about agency: if I am giving some measure of agency in what I do, I will choose to whom I give that agency within the story I'm telling. I chose to use the story of Pen Bascome's murder because I wanted that version of the story made public. Making that story public gave agency because it honored real experience. I chose to use and reframe the Burn story (the woman who cooks her stepmother's food, also in the chapter on reframing) because the reframing incorporated a "capacity to act on one's own behalf." If the woman chooses to make her stepmother's supper, it is a very different feeling from being obliged to do it because nobody else will.

I can give agency in what I write when I can imagine deeply enough to give credence to a story, so I select what I am interested in giving agency to. I select what I can live with in my own being. To write about the Pancake Eater (from The Asterisks section of the "Chaos" chapter), there is a way in which I literally become the pancake eater. Associative imagining and experience do the same things in the body and in energy, and I do some associative imagining to write the stories.*** I do select from a given collection of stories—this is more important—for what I'm interested in making available as agency, "the capacity to act on one's own behalf" in the greater world. That is the first aspect of agency to think about.

The next aspect of agency is also in relation to writing. A character who has agency can say something and it has his/her meaning. Characters who do not have agency say something and it has someone else's meaning. I wrote something of a feminist piece for the Mennonites, not that they would call it that. The play, entitled *Plowing Outback*, was about changing times and changing lives. This community has lost farms and a traditional way of life to strip malls and subdivisions, and the lives of the generation who are raising children now are very different from their parents. The title comes from the fact that an Outback restaurant sits on what was, not very long ago, a field used to raise silage for dairy cows. There is a scene in the play in which the man who used to own that land (and plant and harvest silage from it) is eating dinner at the Outback restaurant. The idea for the scene and for the title of the play came as I ate dinner with him and his wife in that restaurant and listened to their stories.

There is a section in *Plowing Outback* in which four young women who had been friends since childhood (such continuity!) meet for coffee. The young women all carry cell phones. "It is how you raise children in the new millennium," says one of them. Their mothers, also lifelong friends, are on a different part of the stage in an intercut scene that is about some of the changes the Mennonite community has gone through in the last few years. Part of the comedy in the scene had to do with the coming of the telephone to the Mennonite community. The Mennonites had cut trees from their farms, raised the telephone poles and strung the first line themselves. There were twenty-nine families on a single party line at first and it was hard not to know at least some of one another's business.

I wrote a character for the scene who confronted the younger women about the things they no longer kept from the Mennonite tradition, like wearing plain clothes. This character didn't like that they all had jobs outside the home, and that nobody from the community knew what was happening to them anymore because they had all those cell phones. I made the confrontational character comic, because I thought that comedy would help diffuse some of the tension in the community around the issues of what traditions to keep and what to let go. The scene was rejected by the play committee. They liked the play, but they didn't like that character. I wrote a second version of the scene that did essentially the same thing. The confrontation was different, but it was still a comic character doing the confronting. Second rejection. I didn't understand the problem yet. Finally, after some agony on both our parts—theirs especially, they make decisions by consensus— the confrontational character was turned into the grandmother of one of the young women and the jokes were cut. It became a much harder take on the situation, but that was acceptable to them. My lesson: I could go to the difficult questions, the questions were not the problem. It just had to be done by a character who had agency, one who could say "I" and be herself when she said it. Anything less than that was an "I" with no agency, a mouthpiece for something Jo-the-playwright needed to have said to make the scene work. Oh. I was right about what needed to be said in the scene; they were right about who could say it. It had to be a character with agency.

That community and I trust one another's good intentions enough that our relationship was not ruined after that bump. Relationships between artists and communities in this business can be ruined after just one bump like that. But I learned from that experience. At the time, I didn't have this analysis, this "I" with agency is something I see in retrospect. Agency—keeping real agency in mind, being aware of agency, giving agency—is the single most essential element in this work, and maybe in *any* other work as well.

The next aspects of agency are complicated and move the thinking beyond what happens between my computer and me, into the greater world. Ideas have energy or patterns in the zero point field. Remember what the blue-haired lady at Black Mountain was able to do. New ideas make new patterns. Once one person has had an idea, it becomes easier for another to find the same idea, even with no direct communication between the two of them.

The traditional story used to illustrate this is that a monkey on an island learned or was taught to wash food in the ocean before eating it, and soon other monkeys on the same island were washing their food. (The food was some kind of root so it could use the washing.) That part is easy to explain: other monkeys saw the first one and copied her. What is harder to explain is that very soon, monkeys on other islands were washing their edible roots even though there was no transfer of monkeys between the islands. Now, there are arguments in the literature about whether this story is true or not because it was reported, not documented. So, if you don't like the monkeys, how about some mice? These experiments are documented. One mouse figuring out a maze in one place seems to allow another mouse in an identical maze in another place to learn the same maze in a shorter period of time than it took the first, and a third in a shorter period of time than the first two. How?

Much harder to document is what happens in science or the arts, happens over and over again in my experience in the arts. Ideas seem to come into being with more than one person realizing them at very close to the same time. Science is also full of these stories. We have an idiomatic way to speak of this: "an idea whose time has come." Like "anger eating you alive" or "an eye-opening experience," the idiom is interesting for the levels of truth in it.

Rupert Sheldrake calls this phenomenon "morphic resonance" and he came to the idea as a biologist. One of the unsolved mysteries of biology is how cells in a growing organism know what to become as the organism grows: eye, heart, claw . . . An experimenter can transplant cells from a different part of the organism and the right item still grows in the right place. You can even put human DNA in a mouse—splice some mouse out, put some human in—and the mouse still grows into a viable mouse with the right things in the right places. Humans and mice share something like ninety-five percent (you can find slightly different numbers, I'm using a low one) of the same DNA sequence, so this is doable. Here is the question nobody can answer: How did the growing mouse know it was a mouse that needed mouse parts even with the human DNA in it? Sheldrake's theory of morphic resonance says that the pattern for the organism is present in the energy fields that make up the universe, and the growth of an organism follows that pattern. Sheldrake's name for this field is the "morphic field." Zero point field is another name for the same territory.****

And it is the same energy field the woman at Black Mountain was able to tap into. This energy field not only holds the patterns of life in it, so a fetal mouse knows to become a mouse instead of something else, it is also how ideas become available, because they, too, have energy. The monkeys on the other islands learned to wash roots because, once the first monkey had done it, the idea was available in the zero point field. The mice in mazes in different places did the same thing. This is also how scientists or artists (or societies) seem to come onto the same idea at the same time.

The role agency plays is either as the creator of new patterns in the field, or as the revealer of old patterns already available.

Opening possibilities in one being opens those same possibilities for everyone/anyone capable of (or susceptible to) tuning in to the zero point field. (Actually, you can't live without the zero point field, because the field is what holds your personal assortment of changing atoms together as your body—remember the nucleus the size of a single house fly in the middle of Notre Dame Cathedral with all that empty space around it as a description of an atom . . . well, it is a description of the atoms that make up your body, too.) Likewise, a being assuming agency makes that agency available for other beings to assume. Want some real-world examples? Gandhi's practice of nonviolent confrontation was one of the models for Martin Luther King, Jr.'s leadership practices in the civil rights movement. M.L.K. could very well have known about Gandhi's work and never raised a finger. Instead, he assumed the agency and the idea. Rosa Parks sat down on a bus and became a model for many, many more. Edmund Hillary climbed Mt. Everest in 1953 "because it was there." Now, anyone who has enough money, and wants to, can do it. The Vikings sailed the Atlantic to Greenland and beyond. Somebody walked the Bering Straits when an ice bridge was in place. Somebody first ate an oyster. (That took some courage.) Somebody, way back there, stood up on their hind legs and learned to walk. When experience or art (or anything else) gives agency, more of that agency is made available in the zero point field.

Another application of this thinking is in what happens to an individual when a story of his or hers is told, in other words when an experience is validated. The capacity to act on one's own behalf, to say "I" and be somebody specific in the story, creates patterns in the individual's energy field (remember, again, experience is held in energy), and those patterns are reinforced in the telling of a story that has agency. A person with agency can act with even more agency.

The same is true of an experience that robs agency, it feels wretched when it happens and it does equally wretched things to the individual's energy. This gets reinforced in the retelling unless there is some reframing done in a way that adds value beyond wretched experience.*****

Collective agency expressed in the zero point field may lead to the idea of archetypes as energy patterns in human experience. Archetypes themselves are a rather well-established area of study thanks to Jung and his followers, but there is interesting new thinking about how they work in an individual's life. Caroline Myss wrote a how-to book, *Sacred Contracts*, to assist an individual in identifying and using those archetypes in a constructive way.

The next aspect of agency is easy to see in the community story work. A person telling the story of a character who has agency can find himself practicing that agency in rehearsal and, then, find himself becoming capable of expressing agency in his life in a way that may not have been possible before. The same is true of acting a role. Someone called acting "Divine possession" and here is how it works: practicing agency, play-acting agency, opens the possibility of real agency, because it opens a pattern in the individual's energy field.****** The specific examples of this in the story work are almost always small and cumulative. They become most evident in a situation, for example, like that of women in a community where their experience does not have the same (public) value as that of the men's. (The Mennonites are an example, but this is true in most communities.) When I first began working with the Mennonites, women would tell their men's stories if they told stories at all, and most didn't. Finding stories in which women had agency was difficult at first. Ten years later, it is not at all difficult. The Mennonite women do speak for themselves and speak of their own experience. This is very small and very large at the same time. The hardest step in some of these endeavors is getting people to see themselves as having stories of any value at all. Talk about giving agency: finding people's experience valuable is always the premise that starts these projects and it may be the single most important thing that happens.

An example from *Plowing Outback* suggests how agency can be bestowed on an individual by a role. The main character in the play, Effie, was a loose cannon on a very tight ship from the time she was adopted into the community as a child. She was beloved, remembered fondly even after her death, but she was also rather an embarrassment, especially to a younger generation as she got older, because she was so brash. The woman who literally demanded to play the role had been a friend of Effie's. Her inclinations in wanting the part were upfront conservative. She did not want someone misrepresenting her friend onstage. She had not participated in the previous productions in that community and didn't much approve of them; she seemed to feel they made the community too public. It was too much like tooting your own horn. Horn-tooting is not something the Mennonite community is inclined to do. Then, as rehearsal progressed, her demeanor changed, she began to take on some of Effie's chutzpah on and off the stage. Maybe acting really is "Divine possession," or what I'm really suggesting, maybe Effie's energy patterns became available to the woman playing the role.

She set up and played a joke on one of the patriarchs of the community. At the last dress rehearsal, in character, in context, and in public, she dumped flour over the man's head at a moment in the story when his character disapproved of something his wife had done.******* The flour dumping was not something I had written, the gesture would not have passed the consensus committee, it would have been a "forced playwright" moment. It was not something that was directed, either. (I don't think anyone short of God could have directed that.) The woman playing the role found it in her onstage character and did it in keeping with that character. The moment was kept in the public performance because the gesture claimed such agency that it brought the final dress rehearsal to a dead stop. Nothing short of catastrophe stops a final rehearsal in the theater. The astonishment and laughter that followed were too big not to go for again, and everyone knew it. It was a moment that only the woman playing that character could do, and do in public, and do with great joy and fun, having rehearsed and played deep within her character's agency.

We actually use this idea a lot in our culture. We teach agency by role-playing. Psychologists have patients role-play to overcome problems. Employment agencies use role-playing to teach people how to conduct themselves in interviews. We teach parenting to young mothers-to-be through role-playing. Children role-play quite naturally without being aware that they are doing it. The list goes on. Role-playing is different from imitation; it takes a different level of imagining. It can begin in imitation but it has to grow. I think it can even be argued that young animals do more than just imitate adults of their kind; even within the confines of instinctual behavior, they role-play to learn how to behave in their social order and to survive.

It is not possible to draw $A + B = C$ equations out of other people's lives because of their participation in a play, but I have watched people change, speak up, assume agency in the process of these projects. I see this happen for women more often than men, because men usually have more agency to start with, it is awarded to them by this culture. I've seen it work with children, too. In one case, an autistic child was able to say lines in a play in an appropriate way over the course of coming to want to do it. No small trick with autism, that "coming to want to do it." In that situation, "coming to want to do it" is another naming of agency. So maybe the way to think of this story work, the passages past the dragon, the reframings, the energy, everything, all of it, is as a series of how-to(s) for something so simple as giving agency.

We could do worse.

⊰ The Asterisks ⊱

*My use of this story is an odd way to give agency, but it does honor experience, an agency basic. This piece is from a community play, *Crooked Rivers: Sisters Three*. I wrote the piece from a very few lines of an oral history given by a man who found the situation funny. His "crazy" grandmother spent her last years so frightened of other people that she hid behind her closed door and barked like a dog whenever anyone came to her house. I don't find that situation particularly funny; in need of some help, yes, but not funny.

In addition, I broke several of my own rules with this scene (another reason to include it here–breaking rules, especially my own, is a regular source of satisfaction). First, unlike most of what

I write for community plays, it is a scene that asks actors to play roles with no narrative at all. Second, I wasn't true to the oral history as it was told. The original teller made fun of the fear and I didn't do that. However backward and misguided and useless the fear may have been, to belittle it by making fun of it would have been a theft of the old woman's agency. I couldn't change whatever it was that made her so fearful (she is long gone from this world), but I could recognize her fear without making her the butt of a joke. I set up a situation and invented the characters to unfold the situation in an interesting way, and the revelation at the end of the scene created the shock it ought to have onstage. Here is the excerpt:

> *(A front stoop with a door . . . a man or a child, a peddler of some sort, maybe selling band candy, nothing the least bit scary, comes to the door and knocks. Barking comes from behind the closed door. He knocks again, more barking. He waits for a minute, the door does not open, he exits and the barking stops. A pause. Another person, maybe a church lady, comes to the same door, knocks. Barking only. She, too, leaves and the barking stops. A word about the barking: it should be human. It should not be constant, but it should punctuate the scene. We do not ever see the person doing the barking.*
>
> *Two young people come to the steps outside the same door.)*

YOUNG MAN: Nice evening.
YOUNG WOMAN: Oh, yes.
YM: Really good movie.
YW: I loved it.
YM: "Here's looking at you, kid."
YW: You sound just like him.
YM: Will you go with me again? Another movie?
YW: I'd like that very much.
YM: Could we just sit a little?
YW: We can try. It might get a little noisy.

(They are both interested in doing the right thing by each other and pleased to be in one another's company; after a moment, the barking commences.)

YM: Is that your dog?

YW: No.

YM: You live here.

YW: This is my granny's house. Somebody's got to be here right now and I'm the oldest daughter and . . . Well, you know how it is . . . Or maybe you don't. Guys don't usually have to do this kind of thing. Sorry, I don't mean . . . Just say I was available, so I'm here, ok?

YM: I didn't think you grew up around here. I mean I would have seen you before now if you had, I mean I would have noticed you . . . Open mouth, insert foot.

YW: I don't think so.

YM: Well, "here's looking at you" all over again . . .

YW: I'm just from the next county up.

YM: Close enough. *(A pause)* Can't you make that dog hush?

YW: No. Sorry.

YM: It's going crazy in there.

YW: It does that.

YM: It might hush if we let it out.

YW: NO! I mean, it won't come out.

YM: Could we just tie it out back or something?

YW: It wouldn't work.

YM: Kindly gets to you, doesn't it.

YW: Not to me.

YM: Does me.

YW: It is barking at you. It knows me.

YM: I see.

YW: I'm just used to it. Funny what you can get used to if you have to.

YM: I get along pretty good with animals, and if I could just pet it a little . . .

YW: NO!

YM: Well, confound!

YW: It is not a regular dog, ok?

YM: What's wrong with it?

YW: It's crazy.

YM: You should put it down.

YW: No. I mean I can't.

YM: Do it a favor. Crazy isn't fun.

YW: No, it isn't.

YM: What kind of dog is it?

YW: It is just afraid, ok . . .

YM: Afraid of what?

YW: Everything, I think.

YM: That's no life.

YW: I know. You're right. It is old and afraid.

YM: Dogs don't usually get like that unless somebody beats them or something.

YW: I don't know what happened to this one.

YM: Sometimes you can help an animal, even an old dog. It may turn out to be a fear biter. You can't cure aggression, but you can usually get an animal to think a little before it bites something from fear. Even the worst of them.

YW: I think next time we'll just sit somewhere else.

YM: I really could help you with it.

YW: I really don't think there is much help for this one.

YM: Nothing is beyond some help.

YW: I don't know. I don't know what makes anything so afraid. I don't know how you live so afraid. I don't want to ever have to be so afraid. I won't do it. My life won't be like this.

YM: What are you saying?

YW: I think all you have to do to quit being so afraid is just go ahead and die. But I guess that is what there is to be so afraid of, isn't it . . .

YM: What are you talking about?

YW: This old . . . dog. *(A long pause)* When I know you better, I'll tell you more if you want to know, ok?

YM: I'd like to know whatever you want to tell me.

YW: It is not a normal dog. Next movie, we'll just go somewhere else and have a Coke or something . . .

YM: We will go wherever you want.

YW: How about Casablanca?

YM: If that's where you want to go. I really do think I could help you with this dog.

YW: Maybe some day. But not right now.

YM: Well, I guess I better say good night. Before this wakes up the neighborhood.

YW: Wait. (She kisses her fingers and puts her fingers on his lips, a quick, sweet, shy gesture that pleases him very much) Thank you.

YM: Next Saturday? Say yes.

YW: Yes.

(He exits, she watches him go out of sight, out of hearing. Then she goes to the door of the house and speaks through it.)

Grandmother! Granny! Granny! Hush! It is just me out here now. You don't have to be scared anymore . . .

(The barking stops and YW sits on the steps again to just be in the silence a while.)

⊰ ⊱

** The removal of agency in everyday life is one way to think about the –isms (racism or sexism or ageism or classism). The removal of agency in literary endeavors often means that a human is reduced to a stereotype. But stereotyping operates outside literary endeavors, too. No human being on this Earth ever fit a stereotype. Now it can also be said that no human being is entirely free of stereotype either, that stereotypes come from somewhere that has some truth to it, and that by using a stereotype, I simply apply a sort of cultural shorthand. Ok. My tormenters in that motel room were skinheads and Klan goons . . . Fine.

Let me tell another story, this one is from western North Carolina. The woman was in her eighties when she told this; it happened when she was about twenty. She went to help a friend who was incapacitated by a difficult childbirth. Once the new mother became well enough to manage on her own, this young woman was to go home. But when the time came, she was afraid to go. Her father had refused to give her his permission to go help her friend, and she'd gone against his wishes. Her father was inclined to get drunk and abusive when he was angry and he was sure to be angry at her. She told her friend about her worries and she went home. She was met with a beating, but that was something she expected. The problem was that the beating didn't assuage the old man's anger. He hauled his daughter out of the house to the stump where they chopped wood; his plan was to chop off her hands. She fought him and managed to keep him from chopping off any body parts because he was so drunk, but she couldn't get loose from him because she was already hurt. Two men in white sheets came into the yard, they threw a burlap bag of old bones at her father's feet, told him to let her go, and said if anything happened to her, they'd beat him with those same bones. She lived (with both hands) to tell the story. Her friend's husband was one of those men. She felt the Klansmen saved her life.

Didn't expect that, did you? Neither did I. It doesn't fit my stereotype of what Klan behavior was (or is). The story makes me uncomfortable because I know some of the doings the Klan has been (is) party to in the history of racism (and gay-bashing) in this country. Hate crimes are the closest thing I can think of to real evil. I also know what I went through, far more recently than this woman's experience, in that motel room. But a story in which—even just two—Klansmen, however many years ago, were the good guys turns a stereotype I held (and had reinforced in that motel room) on its head. Now, I'm going to make this even harder: the woman who told the story said the Klan was the closest thing women had to police when she was growing up. She said they protected women in that community.

Oh, paradox! (Said like a cuss word.)

It is easier (and far more comfortable) to talk about stereotype in Polish jokes or blond jokes or stories about Jewish mothers or Catholic priests or doctors or lawyers . . . Doctors and blonds don't have an ongoing history of hate crimes.

The point here is that any stereotype is another kind of meme, and it is just as problematic as any other, because it is so likely to be accepted without being questioned.

My thinking about stereotype comes from having spent a significant percentage of my time for the last twenty years reading, and then writing from stories that people tell in oral histories. The time spent doesn't make me an authority but it does give me some experience. Stereotyping is another variety of inattentional blindness; memes almost always contribute to what we are simply not able to see . . .

"She's poor white trash and she's always got another sick baby hanging off of her."

"You know how obtuse black people are . . ."

Etcetera, etcetera.

Stereotype is always applied from outside an individual's experience usually by a dominant culture or way of thinking. A stereotype is most often applied as a way of dismissing or demeaning someone else's experience. A stereotype is never an accurate description of a human condition, because it never comes from the human whose condition is being described. I may not like the condition or attitude of the person I would dismiss with a stereotype, but applying a stereotype is a mistake on my part. Human experience is rich and varied and complex and never easy, and I miss the wealth if I don't pay attention. Applying a stereotype means, very simply, I'm not paying attention.

⊰ ⊱

***This is the magic of trying to write characters that have agency outside of one's own being, a necessity for fiction or drama. The associative imagining necessary to do it is literally an expansion of the experience of the writer. I do not mean that I have literally been that Mennonite family's "pancake eater," but when I sit at my computer and try to imagine what the child who didn't want another pancake felt like when another pancake landed on her plate, I have to *feel* what that might be to write it. And what I feel affects the energy of my body and my being. Essentially, I have had the experience.

This is the best reason I know to teach creative writing. It is not that we need more novels on the market, but creative writing is an exercise in empathy. We have an interesting idiom here, too: "to walk a mile in someone else's shoes." Trying to write a character (other than oneself) is to put on someone else's shoes and try to learn to walk in them. The writing that comes of it may be awful but that's not even the point. The point is to try to imagine someone else's condition deeply enough to be able to speak credibly from it. I teach a playwriting class occasionally at the university here, and much of what I end up trying to teach is how to achieve some level of empathy with someone other than oneself. It comes far easier for some than others (it also seems to come easier at some ages than others) but you can't write characters without that capacity to *feel* beyond yourself. And the moment you can feel beyond yourself, you have literally expanded your own experience. Welcome to one of the more astonishing of the human conditions . . .

⊰ ⊱

****Namings: Reading science can be confusing because people don't always use the same names for what seem to be the same phenomenon. There are several reasons. People want their naming to be the one that sticks. To name something is a way to claim it: claim discovery or claim a measure of understanding. Having other people accept your naming is an acknowledgment of standing in the field (another aspect of agency). Some of the history of science is a series of fights about who knew what and when, and naming is one way to stake out territory. Investigators—especially in the "oscillating possibilities" business—don't yet fully understand what it is they may be trying to name, so you can get different names sometimes from people who are working in the same territory.

The mind-body medicine field is so competitive—I hope it is competitive and not just obtuse—that you get language on the order of this: "I'll call this energy necessary for life 'L-energy.'" Well, it just happens that particular concept of energy has accepted, meaningful names (three I know of, with some variations in spelling, from three different languages, which is confusing enough: "ki" or "qi," "chi" or "ch'i," and "prana") all of which have a history of usage from (at least) the time of Christ. That author is *not* staking out new territory, and a reader who wants to know more about "L-energy" has been done a considerable disservice by the presumption. You can find useful information about "ki" or "qi," "chi" or "ch'i," and "prana" on the internet. Hunting for "L-energy" is like heading down a rabbit hole.

Keep the naming problems in mind if you head into the Further Practice sections of this book.

⊰ ⊱

*****An example of lack of agency: think of me in the motel room with my tormenters at the door. It felt awful, but it has value for me now because I actually stood up for myself. "I quit," was a way to act decisively on my own behalf in that ongoing situation. (It ain't Clint Eastwood's style, but then, I ain't Clint Eastwood, thank you, and the movies often have a very strange take on what real agency might or might not be.) There is actually more to my motel story, and the second part occurred some years later.

I was helping a friend who was in an ongoing difficult situation. I gave her a place to come to when she was upset or afraid, usually both. She'd hide her car a block away in an overgrown alley and walk to my house. Her husband threatened to kill me if I didn't stop taking her in at my house. The threat was not made to my face, he made the threat to her. (He threatened her, too, it was the major reason she showed up at my house to begin with.) The threat against me was likely just big talk said in anger, but she called and told me about it. Fear washed over me. I remembered myself in that motel room and the fear I had felt then. He began stalking me, sitting in his car around the corner from my house, and following me if I went somewhere. I was frightened by this behavior. The stalking went on for two days. On the third day, he appeared again in the rearview mirror of my car, sitting behind me at a stoplight. Instead of cowering as I was supposed to, I faced him down. It was awkward and I tied up traffic when the light turned green. He was stuck in line. Car horns honked behind us. I turned to look him in the eye and then, I waved to him. The stalking stopped.

Assuming the agency to say, "I quit," those years before was on the direct path to looking that man in the eye and waving at him. I know because I felt the "I quit" moment of decision when I did it. It was the web of memory in operation, but with agency included in it. So I waved. I can tell you how I felt when I did both of those things: I felt joyous, absolutely joyous.

⊰ ⊱

******A perfectly unscientific example of this bestowal-of-agency-by-a-role-business comes from a local third-grade class-room, so this is not a situation from one of the community pro-jects. A teacher was using storybooks in her class as supplemental reading material. She had her students doing more than just read-ing the storybooks, they acted some of the stories out in class with the children taking all the roles. I asked her to try something: to cast against type intentionally when she assigned roles (an exam-ple would be to give a shy child a gregarious role), and just to notice if the child's behavior changed in any way besides just dur-ing the play-acting. She said it did seem to make some difference; that a shy child given a gregarious role seemed to participate more in class, at least for the rest of that day. She set about figuring how she could reinforce this new agency for her students. There is no documentation here, and no follow-up with the children to see if that agency carried over at home or in the rest of their activities. It was simply a good teacher's observation, which came out of try-ing an idea, but I was not the least bit surprised by what she reported.

⊰ ⊱

*******This is the story from *Plowing Outback* in which the flour got dumped. In this scene, the character Effie is onstage with the four younger women, they are having coffee; they've made tea for

Effie. Throughout the play, Effie makes dinner rolls. The real woman was famous for her rolls, and almost equally famous for the mess she made making them. She seemed to use making rolls as "comfort work," so every time the character Effie is upset during the play, there is flour flying everywhere because she makes rolls again *right now*. The character Effie has brought rolls to the younger women's get-together. She insists they eat them. They are being gracious and eating her excellent rolls, it doesn't take much effort. Effie is telling a story about the mother of one of the younger women . . .

> EFFIE *(To the young women)*: It was your mother and it was a blizzard . . . eat another roll!
>
> *(Effie is joined onstage by the Woman Who Bought the Chains—WWBTC—as though they were in the front seat of a car.)*

> WWBTC *(To Effie)*: This is more snow than I expected . . .
>
> EFFIE: And it was a lot of snow. We were sliding badly on the road. *(To WWBTC)* Maybe we should just go home . . .
>
> WWBTC: This is my shopping day, getting the car another day is a problem.
>
> EFFIE: We need a set of chains.
>
> WWBTC: Oh! I have a new Esso credit card. We can get chains at the Esso station.
>
> EFFIE *(To the young women)*: And so we went to the Esso station.
>
> WWBTC: We need some chains on our tires.
>
> EFFIE: And they put us on that lift thing that raised us way up in the air and they put chains on our tires. They let us back down and she handed them the new credit card, she signed the little ticket, and we drove out of there without paying any money. We had the best time. We went anywhere we wanted to go. We did our shopping, we had the groceries in

the car, but we helped push people, we helped pull them, we had chains so we could go wherever we wanted and we used them. Your mother wasn't afraid to try anything and it may have been the best day I ever spent in an automobile that I wasn't driving. But then, she got back home.

(WWBTC leaves the car, she's handed a bag of groceries to carry, and approaches her husband.)

And your father had been worried . . .
HUSBAND: Where on earth have you been?
WWBTC: Oh, we were fine, I bought chains for the car.
HUSBAND: Well, if that's how you want to spend your grocery money . . .
WWBTC: I didn't spend grocery money, I charged them.
EVERY MAN IN THE CAST, INCLUDING THE HUSBAND: YOU WHAT?

The actress playing Effie broke the scene here, recovered her prop bag of flour, walked over to the husband and dumped flour from the bag on his head. She said nothing, she just dumped the flour. She then walked back and rejoined the scene with the four young women.

WWBTC: I charged them. You want to eat, don't you? I still had to buy groceries.
EFFIE: And his mouth flattened out to a single line. You could have put a carpenter's level on it. Except it was still snowing. And by the morning, he had to have that car with chains to get the milk trucks out. Had to have it for the next two weeks. He would have been in sad shape without those chains. Now, did he ever say he was glad she charged those chains? He did not. But she had started a revolution.
JANET: How was that a revolution?

EFFIE: She made a financial decision without consulting him, that's how. Next thing she's going to want to know is how much money is in the bank account.

JANET: You think she didn't already know?

EFFIE *(A pause)*: Money is not a good subject for tea. Eat another roll. In my experience, you don't talk about anything real at tea, you make polite conversation.

ELLEN: We usually end up talking about children.

EFFIE: Talk about children is as real as talk about money and they're both too hard to be polite conversation. Church is good. Preachers are excellent. I always did like a good-looking one. That preacher we've got now, we should cover him up with a curtain. He'd be much better if we didn't have to look at him. Excellent tea conversation.

Further Practice

ABOUT MORPHIC RESONANCE . . .

Sheldrake, Ph.D., Rupert. *A New Science of Life: The Hypothesis of Morphic Resonance.*

This lays out Sheldrake's ideas. He is a revolutionary. Sheldrake has a website, sheldrake.org, that is worth a visit and some time spent reading.

The Stories

The Klan story was collected by The Blue Ridge Reading Team (Spruce Pine, North Carolina) and published in a collection of oral histories called *Stories Worth Telling.* Judy Carson (my cousin) worked with The Blue Ridge Reading Team and told me the story.

MAKING ART

MAKING ART OF ANY KIND with any consistency is a mix
of technical skill and the intuitive. If you are really lucky,
art can be practiced, at least for a while, intuitively. Openness to
the intuitive is *the* necessity. I can't write without it. I have no idea
where Pen Bascome's Pearly Gates sermon came from except that
I'd been reading *The Tibetan Book of the Dead*. I knew I needed to use
the story because it had come up several times while I was collecting stories in the community. I knew I needed to reframe it if
I was going to use it, but I had no idea how. I knew a little about
the community. I had been there, I knew a bunch of other stories, I knew the Presbyterian Church has the gold finger that
points to God on the steeple, but I didn't know what I was going
to do with that story until I was sitting at the computer with the
intention and hope and everything else you bring when you look
at the blank page (Ok, blank computer screen), and a character
said, "Maybe that Sunday morning, I'm going to preach a sermon." He made a decision: I can write a story. The rest of the "sermon" wrote itself. I was more like the secretary than the writer.
The crafting came in getting to the moment when the character
could say, "Maybe that Sunday morning . . ." It came like it did,

and it could come, because I know that sometimes the best thing I can do is to let my fingers do the talking.

I know we are better practitioners of any art if we have some technical skill to go with the intuitive. For me, a writer, knowing a little about how to handle the language greases the chutes that carry the intuitive stuff onto the page.

"Write every day without hope and without despair." Isak Dinesen said it, and I think of it differently now than when a favorite professor first admonished me with that instruction. I think it says, "Hold intent; hope and despair are both distractions." I like Flannery O'Connor's thinking: she described herself as sitting at her writing desk every morning from nine till twelve. "Sometimes," she said, "I just sit, but if an idea comes between nine and twelve in the morning, I'm there to get it." She is holding open a dynamic possibility, and bless her, she's funny.

Me, I try to keep the chutes greasy.

The idea of alchemy, turning lead to gold or pain to meaning, is not new to art. It has driven the language arts since the impulse to those arts began. (It may be a different story for the visual arts: think of the cave paintings. Their use was probably in intent; it was to call those animals needed for food to the hunters.) This "pain to meaning" alchemy goes in and out of fashion, but even the keeping of pain (read: "writing about endless misery," fashionable in some fiction these days) refers to the alchemical by the lack of transformation. So the idea of a passage past a dragon or a reframing of a story is anything but new. The truth is that it is likely to be thought just a tad naive right now. Here may be what saves me: I am not the least bit interested in drawing some kind of moral lesson with what I write. With the Burn story in which the woman fixes her stepmother's food, the idea that the woman finds revenge in what looks to be a kindness is an uncomfortable sort of justice at best, but coming to love her duty (for whatever reason) is far better for her body and her being than hating the duty and despising herself for doing it.

With the Pen Bascome Pearly Gates sermon, the character who is making that imaginary sermon that imaginary Sunday morning is compelled by needing some situation in which the murderer has to tell the truth and, as best he can see, it wasn't going to happen in this world. He is right. He also has a belief system in which, just maybe, it can happen in the next world, and he also has intent. This was easier to see onstage because the sermon was delivered to just one person (the man who asks the questions), but if you read the sermon carefully, you'll know the murderer isn't dead yet. His death and the possible public preaching of this sermon are in the future.

Years later, by the time I wrote the sermon, the murderer who was eventually elected sheriff was also dead. He did not ever change his version of events–shooting Pen Bascome in self-defense–as published in the local paper, and the public preaching of the sermon that tells the other version of the story is in a play I wrote. No easy moral there, or at least not one I can find. A reframing, yes. A moral, no.

Here is the rest of the story, and here is why I wrote that sermon like I did: Pen Bascome was not quite dead all those years ago when he was carried home after being shot. The Reverend Pen Bascome, a preacher in his community (another reason I used a sermon format), had nothing more to lose by telling the truth. He died a few hours after he was shot. He was probably shot because he owned land; he'd bought a small farm with a loan from a program especially for black families. It was good, productive land. His family lost the land shortly after Pen Bascome died in a series of local courthouse events that were just as crooked and wretched as his murder. (I used the rest of this story in another place in the play.) If the hospital in the town had served the black community when Pen Bascome was shot he might have lived. Pen Bascome told the sermon version of the story, that he was shot with no provocation, before he died. A spin doctor, the white murderer who later got elected sheriff, had changed the story, and it was the changed story that was accepted. This is why the pain, the injustice, of the event still had such life in the community.

Another of my reasons for handling that story the way I did was to honor the situation that the people who knew Pen Bascome found themselves in at the time of the shooting.

Reporting the real story truly might have gotten someone else shot. They would have been "making trouble." I find this "making trouble" business another big, true, ongoing undercurrent in many situations, not that getting shot is always the bottom line. I was harassed in the motel room for what someone perceived as "making trouble." Collecting old stories is making trouble? Well, it can be. It depends on who wants to protect what. If you needed further proof that stories carry energy in a community, this is it. And collecting stories is perceived as "making trouble" more often than you might imagine. Pen Bascome and the man who killed him (and was eventually elected sheriff) were both long dead by the time I got to telling that story, but layer upon layer of human experience is folded and enfolded again in that story. Many, many stories are enfolded like that. Their permutations are, like universes, endless.

I write at my computer, Bear Dog is often on the rug at the door of my study. She pays attention and barks when I start talking out loud. I am a noisy writer, I have to try out those things to be spoken aloud in order to know how they work, and she is an equally noisy critic. She makes me laugh because she is more adamant in her barking when I get the emotion and rhythm of an exchange I'm writing (and also speaking aloud) right. I really get barked at if I'm talking angry. And she's right, I should be barked at. I can't afford much angry talking.

When I am writing stories or essays, I am responsible to myself and to my readers, but I write mostly for the theater. For theater to happen, it takes other artists besides me: directors, designers, actors who all share responsibility for what happens in a production and, then, an audience to whom we are all responsible. When I am writing for an event made from the stories of other people's lives, it takes those artists and many, many other people in the place the stories come from to make the event happen. When the audience who sees the event has their own investment in the stories, I am writing for something different than what we usually think of as theater. I think our stories should be (at least some of) our theater. I think that because of what I've seen happen in communities when their stories are used. So much of the entertainment business creates "art" as some kind of escape. Too many shamans are throwing away their tools. Making art truly local is a way to recover some of those tools.

I do understand what good traditional theater can do and I love it. (I write for it, too.) I also know the value of entertainment, and if Mennonite women fall out of their seats laughing when the character Effie dumps her flour, that actress with agency, the rest of the team, and I have done our job right. I am compelled by the community work because there is nothing else that accomplishes for people what happens in the process of making art that they understand as relevant to their lives and their communities. These events have all the hazards that come with lots of people (we had one hundred and forty people onstage in one production, another with ninety, fifty is closer to the norm), and those hazards are more than plenty, but these events have intent working for them as well, and they can be stunning.

When I am writing for these community events, I am the architect. I'm the one who takes what is available and, by what I can imagine, I give a play content and structure. I want, I need, I hope, I intend to know, on multiple levels, what in this world I am doing.

PARADOX

So I've wrapped up art. Now, I'm supposed to wrap up what I've said about energy and stories, and draw cogent conclusions about human well-being, storytelling and quantum physics.

I don't have those conclusions. Consider it the same sort of paradox the rest of this universe seems to be made of.

I don't have conclusions because conclusions close things, and I don't want this closed. I want ongoing speculations. I want to have opened a dynamic process with this work, one that is available to the flutter of butterfly wings and the doings of Tricksters.

To speculate on something is to meditate on it. Speculation is "contemplation of a profound nature," but my pretense ("a right asserted with or without foundation") to profundity is in "penetrating beyond what is superficial or obvious." So *The American Heritage Dictionary* tells me.

So call this foray "one writer's meditations, so far, beyond what is obvious in storytelling." You can even call it "one writer's obsessive meditations." I don't mind.

And you can call this the end of a beginning, but please don't call it a conclusion.

For me to pretend (again, that right asserted with or without foundation) that I have come to an end of what there is to say would be to close my eyes to further possibility, and that is the last thing I want to do. I've just barely opened them.

At the turn of the twentieth century, there were a series of announcements by eminent scientists of the time who truly believed that all that could be known about physics was already known. There was nothing further that anyone could ever possibly uncover. And they said this, out loud, and in print. It was a *relatively* large mistake. To assume there is nothing more to say about energy and the stories of our lives, how we live with them and use them, and what they do for us and in us, would be a similar mistake.

So, no conclusions.

Instead, consider an invitation. Assume agency and use these ideas. Try them and figure out how to see and to *feel* what happens. Play (I mean really big play) and enjoy.

If you find stories you'd like to report, I'd love to see them. You can reach me on that other web, the world wide one:

spiderspeculations@gmail.com

Invoking Spider always helps in the making and using of stories.

FURTHER PRACTICE

A Bibliography

I'VE LISTED BOOKS that were important to my learning. This is not the whole of my (ongoing) reading list, but these are the ones that were useful for this book. Most of these books have already been noted in the Further Practice sections with each of the chapters. This list includes those books, but it also includes a few others that had no specific application to these speculations but were also useful to my learning. I would also suggest watching *What the Bleep Do We Know?*, an independent film by William Arntz, Betty Chasse and Mark Vicente, released in 2004 and available on DVD.

The books in this list are grouped loosely by subject matter or discipline. There is, of course, some overlap among them. Expect it.

This list is somewhat different from what you've found in the Further Practice sections at the end of chapters. At the end of the chapters, I listed books according to *how they served my learning for that chapter*: "About So-and-So." Here, you may not find So-and-So, but you will find the books listed under their proper discipline (or subject matter). At the ends of the chapters, you also found notes about the books. Those notes are not here either. This is just the books, ma'am, just the books . . .

Reading is wonderful but reading is not experience. If you want energy experience (Is it happening to you yet?) go to an energy practitioner. Even better, learn some energy-healing endeavor yourself. It is a human capacity; some of us are better at it than others, true, but we can all do it. Then do some hands-on work yourself. It is, at the very least, a kindness to your fellow beings. With luck, it might be your knock of the spirit.

And one final note: there are better and lesser writers included in this list. Some folks put words in order in more compelling ways than others. The ability to write about experience or learning is not necessarily a measure of the value of the experience or of the learning being reported.

ARCHETYPES

Jung, C. G. *Man and His Symbols.* Garden City, NY: Doubleday & Company, 1964.

Myss, Ph.D., Caroline. *Sacred Contracts: Awakening Your Divine Potential.* New York: Harmony Books, 2001.

Turnbull, Ph.D., Sharon. *Goddess Gift: Discover Your Personal Goddess Type.* Marina del Rey, CA: Quiet Time Press, 2006.

BEAR

Jenkins, Ken L. *Black Bear Reflections.* Merrillville, IN: ICS Books, 1995.

Rockwell, David B. *Giving Voice to Bear: American Indian Myths, Rituals, and Images of the Bear.* Lanham, MD: Roberts Rinehart, 2003.

Shepard, Paul and Barry Sanders. *The Sacred Paw: The Bear in Nature, Myth, and Literature.* New York: Viking, 1985.

BUDDHISM/MEDITATION

His Holiness the Dalai Lama, translated by Jeffery Hopkins, Ph.D., *How to Practice: The Way to a Meaningful Life*. New York: Pocket Books, 2002.

Kornfield, Jack. *After the Ecstasy, the Laundry: How the Heart Grows Wise on the Spiritual Path*. New York: Bantam Books, 2000.

Thurman, Robert A. F. *Essential Tibetan Buddhism*. San Francisco: HarperSanFrancisco, 1995.

_____. *The Tibetan Book of the Dead* (translation). New York: Bantam Books, 1994.

Thurman, Robert A. F. and Tad Wise. *Circling the Sacred Mountain: A Spiritual Adventure Through the Himalayas*. New York: Bantam Books, 1999.

CHAOS

Briggs, John. *Fractals—The Patterns of Chaos: Discovering a New Aesthetic of Art, Science, and Nature*. New York: Simon & Schuster, 1992.

Gladwell, Malcolm. *The Tipping Point: How Little Things Can Make a Big Difference*. Boston: Back Bay Books, 2002.

Gleick, James. *Chaos: Making a New Science*. New York: Penguin, 1987.

Walter, Ph.D., Katya. *Tao of Chaos: Merging East and West*. Austin, TX: Kairos Center, 1994.

Wheatley, Margaret J. *Leadership and the New Science: Discovering Order in a Chaotic World*. San Francisco: Berrett-Koehler, 2006.

CHRISTIAN TRADITION

Barnstone, Willis, editor. *The Other Bible*. San Francisco: HarperSanFrancisco, 1984.

Leloup, Jean-Yves (translated from the Coptic and commentaries) and Joseph Rowe (English translation). *The Gospel of Mary Magdalene*. Rochester, VT: Inner Traditions, 2002.

Mack, Burton L. *The Lost Gospel: The Book of Q and Christian Origins*. San Francisco: HarperSanFrancisco, 1993.

Pagels, Elaine. *Adam, Eve, and the Serpent*. New York: Random House, 1988.

_____. *The Gnostic Gospels*. New York: Vintage Books, 1981.

_____. *The Origin of Satan*. New York: Random House, 1996.

COMPLEXITY

Waldrop, M. Mitchell. *Complexity: The Emerging Science at the Edge of Order and Chaos*. New York: Simon & Schuster, 1992.

DOWSING

Grace, Raymon. *The Future Is Yours: Do Something About It*. Self-published, the book can be purchased from Raymon Grace's website: RaymonGrace.com.

Webster, Richard. *Dowsing for Beginners: The Art of Discovering: Water, Treasure, Gold, Oil, Artifacts*. St. Paul, MN: Llewellyn Publications, 1996.

DREAMS AND USING DREAMS

Barasch, Marc Ian. *Healing Dreams: Exploring the Dreams That Can Transform Your Life*. New York: Riverhead Books, 2000.

Cayce, Edgar. Jess Stern and numerous others have written about Cayce and his work as a healer and a visionary.

Elk, Black, as told to John G. Niehardt. *Black Elk Speaks*. New York: William Morrow & Company, 1932.

THE ENERGY BODY AND HEALING

Brennan, Barbara Ann. *Hands of Light: A Guide to Healing Through the Human Energy Field: A New Paradigm for the Human Being in Health, Relationship, and Disease*. New York: Pleiades Books, 1987.

_____. *Light Emerging: The Journey of Personal Healing.* New York: Bantam Books, 1993.

Bruyere, Rosalyn L. *Wheels of Light: A Study of the Chakras.* Sierra Madre, CA: Bon Productions, 1989.

Chopra, M.D., Deepak. *Quantum Healing: Exploring the Frontiers of Mind/Body Medicine.* New York: Bantam Books, 1989.

Eden, Donna with David Feinstein. *Energy Medicine: Balance Your Body's Energies for Optimal Health, Joy, and Vitality.* New York: Jeremy P. Tarcher/Putnam, 1998.

Gordon, Richard. *Quantum-Touch: The Power to Heal.* Berkeley, CA: North Atlantic Books, 2006.

Hay, Louise L. *Heal Your Body A–Z: The Mental Causes for Physical Illness and the Way to Overcome Them.* Carlsbad, CA: Hay House, 1998.

Hunt, Ph.D., Valerie V. *Infinite Mind: Science of the Human Vibrations of Consciousness.* Malibu, CA: Malibu Publishing Co., 1996.

Myss, Ph.D., Caroline M. *Anatomy of the Spirit: The Seven Stages of Power and Healing.* New York: Harmony Books, 1996.

_____. *Why People Don't Heal and How They Can.* New York: Harmony Books, 1997.

Myss, Ph.D., Caroline M. with Norman C. Shealy, M.D. *The Creation of Health: The Emotional, Psychological, and Spiritual Responses That Promote Health and Healing.* New York: Three Rivers Press, 1998.

Pearsall, M.D., Paul. *The Heart's Code: Tapping the Wisdom and Power of Our Heart Energy.* New York: Broadway Books, 1998.

Stein, Diane. *Essential Reiki: A Complete Guide to an Ancient Healing Art.* Freedom, CA: Crossing Press, 1995.

HEALING WITH SOUND

Ashley-Farrand, Thomas. *Healing Mantras: Using Sound Affirmations for Personal Power, Creativity, and Healing.* New York: Ballantine Wellspring, 1999.

Goldman, Jonathan. *Healing Sounds: The Power of Harmonics.* Rochester, VT: Healing Arts Press, 2002.

_____. Numerous CDs from Spirit Music.

Huna

Long, Max Freedom. *The Secret Science Behind Miracles.* Los Angeles: Huna Research Publications, 1954.

Intent

Braden, Gregg. *The Isaiah Effect: Decoding the Lost Science of Prayer and Prophecy.* New York: Harmony Books, 2000.

Burnham, Sophy. *The Path of Prayer: Reflections on Prayer and True Stories of How It Affects Our Lives.* New York: Viking Compass, 2002.

Byrne, Rhonda. *The Secret.* New York: Atria Books, 2006

Dossey, M.D., Larry. *Healing Words: The Power of Prayer and the Practice of Medicine.* San Francisco: HarperSanFrancisco, 1993

Dyer, Dr. Wayne W. *The Power of Intention: Learning to Co-create Your World.* Carlsbad, CA: Hay House, 2004.

Emoto, Masauru, translated by David A. Ihayne. *The Hidden Messages in Water.* Hillsboro, OR: Beyond Words Publishing, 2004.

Herrigel, Eugen. *Zen in the Art of Archery.* New York: Vintage Books, 1989.

Tiller, Ph.D., William; Dibble, Jr., Ph.D., Walter and Michael Kohane, Ph.D. *Conscious Acts of Creation: The Emergence of a New Physics.* Walnut Creek, CA: Pavior Publications, 2001.

Wilson, Robert Anton. *Prometheus Rising.* Tempe, AZ: New Falcon Publications, 1983.

Memes

Balkin, J. M. *Cultural Software: A Theory of Ideology.* New Haven, CT: Yale University Press, 1998.

Brodie, Richard. *Virus of the Mind: The New Science of the Meme.* Seattle: Integral Press, 1996.

NLP REFRAMING

Bandler, Richard and John Grinder. *ReFraming: Neuro-Linguistic Programming and the Transformation of Meaning.* Moab, UT: Real People Press, 1982.

OUT-OF-THE-BODY EXPERIENCE

Monroe, Robert A. *Journeys Out of the Body.* Garden City, NY: Doubleday, 1971.

PERCEPTION

Gladwell, Malcolm. *Blink: The Power of Thinking Without Thinking.* New York: Back Bay Books, 2007.

Grandin, Temple and Catherine Johnson. *Animals in Translation: Using the Mysteries of Autism to Decode Animal Behavior.* Orlando, FL: Harcourt, 2006.

PLAY

Ackerman, Diane. *Deep Play.* New York: Random House, 1999.

REINCARNATION

Shroder, Thomas. *Old Souls: The Evidence for Past Lives.* New York: Simon & Schuster, 1999.

RELATED PHILOSOPHY

Hubbard, Barbara Marx. *Conscious Evolution: Awakening Our Social Potential.* Navato, CA: New World Library, 1998.

Hyde, Lewis. *The Gift: Imagination and the Erotic Life of Property.* New York: Vintage Books, 1983.

Jaynes, Julian. *The Origins of Consciousness in the Breakdown of the Bicameral Mind.* New York: Houghton Mifflin, 2000.

Wilber, Ken A. *Theory of Everything: An Integral Vision for Business, Politics, Science and Spirituality.* Boston: Shambhala Publications, 2000.

THE SCIENCE

Bryson, Bill. *A Short History of Nearly Everything.* New York: Broadway Books, 2005.

Greene, Brian. *The Elegant Universe: Superstrings, Hidden Dimensions, and the Quest for the Ultimate Theory.* New York: Vintage Books, 1999.

_____. *The Fabric of the Cosmos: Space, Time, and the Texture of Reality.* New York: Vintage Books, 2004.

Hawking, Ph.D., Stephen. *A Brief History of Time: From the Big Bang to Black Holes.* New York: Bantam Books, 1988.

McTaggart, Lynne. *The Field: The Quest for the Secret Force of the Universe.* New York: HarperCollins, 2002.

_____. *The Intention Experiment: Using Your Thoughts to Change Your Life and the World.* New York: Free Press, 2007.

Pert, Ph.D., Candace B. *Molecules of Emotion: The Science Behind Mind-Body Medicine.* New York: Scribner, 1997.

_____. "Your Body Is Your Subconscious Mind," audio CD. Boulder, CO: Sounds True, 2004.

Pribram, M.D., Karl. "The Holographic Brain," DVD. Berkeley, CA: Thinking Allowed Productions.

Sheldrake, Ph.D., Rupert. *Dogs That Know When Their Owners Are Coming Home and Other Unexplained Powers of Animals.* New York: Crown Publishing, 1999

_____. *A New Science of Life: The Hypothesis of Morphic Resonance.* Rochester, VT: Parkstreet Press, 1995.

_____. *Seven Experiments That Could Change the World: A Do-It-Yourself Guide to Revolutionary Science.* Rochester, VT: Parkstreet Press, 2002.

Smolin, Lee. *The Life of the Cosmos.* New York: Oxford University Press, 1997

Talbot, Michael. *The Holographic Universe.* New York: Harper-Collins Publishers, 1991.

_____. *Mysticism and the New Physics.* London: Arkana, 1993.

Wilber, Ken, editor. *The Holographic Paradigm and Other Paradoxes: Exploring the Leading Edge of Science.* Boston: Shambhala Publications, 1982.

Zukav, Gary. *The Dancing Wu Li Masters: An Overview of the New Physics.* New York: Harper Perennial, 2001.

SHAMANISM

Harner, Michael J. *The Way of the Shaman: A Guide to Power and Healing.* San Francisco: Harper & Row, 1980.

Villoldo, Ph.D., Alberto and Stanley Krippner, Ph.D. *Healing States: A Journey into the World of Spiritual Healing and Shamanism.* New York: Simon & Schuster, 1987.

Vitebsky, Piers. *The Shaman.* Boston: Little, Brown and Company, 1995.

STORY, STORYTELLING, STORY WORK

Bruner, Jerome. *Actual Minds, Possible Worlds.* Cambridge, MA: Harvard University Press, 1986.

_____. *Making Stories: Law, Literature and Life.* New York: Farrar, Straus & Giroux, 2002.

Frank, Arthur W. *The Wounded Storyteller: Body, Illness, and Ethics.* Chicago: University of Chicago Press, 1995.

Goffman, Erving. *The Presentation of Self in Everyday Life*. London: Allen Lane, 1969.

Kleinman, M.D., Arthur. *The Illness Narratives: Suffering, Healing & the Human Condition*. New York: Basic Books, 1988.

Lakoff, George and Mark Johnson. *Metaphors We Live By*. Chicago: University of Chicago Press, 1980.

McAdams, Dan P. *The Stories We Live By: Personal Myths and the Making of the Self*. New York: William Morrow & Company, 1993.

Stone, Richard. *The Healing Art of Storytelling: A Sacred Journey of Personal Discovery*. New York: Hyperion, 1996.

SYNCHRONICITY

Combs, Allan and Mark Holland. *Synchronicity: Science, Myth, and the Trickster*. New York: Marlow & Co., 1996.

Hopcke, Robert H. *There Are No Accidents: Synchronicity and the Stories of Our Lives*. New York: Riverhead Books, 1997.

Jung, C. G. *Synchronicity: An Acausal Connecting Principle*. New York: Routledge, 1985.

TOLTEC (ENERGY) TRADITION

Abelar, Taisha. *The Sorcerer's Crossing: A Woman's Journey*. New York: Viking Arkana, 1992.

Castaneda, Carlos.

(Books are listed in order of suggested reading, chronological order.)

The Teachings of don Juan: A Yaqui Way of Knowledge. New York: Simon & Schuster, 1973. (First published by University of California Press in 1968.)

A Separate Reality. New York: Simon & Schuster, 1971.

Journey to Ixtlan. New York: Simon & Schuster, 1972.

Tales of Power. New York: Simon & Schuster, 1974.

The Second Ring of Power. New York: Simon & Schuster, 1979.

The Eagle's Gift. New York: Simon & Schuster, 1981.

The Fire from Within. New York: Simon & Schuster, 1984.

The Power of Silence. New York: Simon & Schuster, 1987.

The Art of Dreaming. New York: HarperCollins, 1993.

The Active Side of Infinity. New York: HarperCollins, 1998.

Donner, Florinda. *Being-in-Dreaming: An Initiation into the Sorcerors' World.* San Francisco: HarperSanFrancisco, 1991.

_____. *The Witch's Dream: A Healer's Way of Knowledge.* New York: Simon & Schuster, 1985.

Nelson, Mary Carroll. *Beyond Fear—A Toltec Guide to Freedom and Joy: The Teachings of don Miguel Ruiz.* Tulsa, OK: Council Oak Books, 1997.

Ruiz, M.D., Miguel. *The Four Agreements: A Practical Guide to Personal Freedom.* San Rafael, CA: Amber-Allen Publishing, 1997.

Sanchez, Victor. *The Toltec Path of Recapitulation: Healing Your Past to Free Your Soul.* Rochester, VT: Bear & Company, 2001.

Wallace, Amy. *Sorcerer's Apprentice: My Life with Carlos Castaneda.* Berkeley, CA: Frog Books, 2003.

TRANSPLANT EXPERIENCES

Sylvia, Claire with William Novak. *A Change of Heart: A Memoir.* Boston: Little, Brown & Company, 1997.

TRICKSTER

Erdoes, Richard and Alfonso Ortiz. *American Indian Trickster Tales.* New York: Viking, 1998.

Hyde, Lewis. *Trickster Makes This World: Mischief, Myth and Art.* New York: Farrar, Straus & Giroux, 1998.

WRITING

O'Connor, Flannery, selected and edited by Sally and Robert Fitz-gerald. *Mystery and Manners.* New York: Farrar, Straus & Giroux, 1969.

ACKNOWLEDGMENTS

THE THANKS ARE MANY, and acknowledgments beyond just thanks are in order.

Joe Benton, Roe Bear, Sylvia Lagergren and Joe Ortola (Reiki masters, all) have been essential to my learning about the energy work. Their generosity with answers to my questions and further questions in useful directions is more than appreciated. Lee Parton (the man who "hearts" higher math) took the pain away that first time. This list is actually much, much longer: Irwin Yacker (a healer who used prayer), Raymon Grace (a dowser), Dr. M. A. Filka (Sufi), Fay Campbell, Paula Sarut . . . Also: a web group, the color seer I met in Colorado, the woman at Black Mountain, the man who could (briefly) let my ears work like they are supposed to, and many others have contributed to my learning. I've found the energy-healing community truly generous, and thanks to a few people at the back of the book is hardly more than a nod in the right direction.

David James did the dowsing demonstration recounted in the book.

Constance V. Douglas, APRN, Psych/Mental Health, B.C., and Sharon Turnbull, Ph.D. have been truly helpful with medical and psychological insights and resources for my thinking. Dr.

Turnbull has a website about exploring archetypes. I recommend it: goddessgift.com.

Skip Carson, my brother, has served as neurolinguistic programming consultant. His knowledge has enriched this endeavor considerably.

The book has been through several iterations with a series of readers who have all helped clarify my thinking. Beyond the Reiki masters (listed above) and medical people (also listed above), the list includes: Paul Bowen, Lisa Mount, Loren Chapman and Kathie de Nobriga. This necessary-for-clarification-reader-list also includes Dr. Joseph Sobol. You will find Joe Sobol on the web; he's a fine storyteller himself and head of the storytelling department at East Tennessee State University. He said, among many other things, that my reading was omnivorous. I stole the line.

Sandy Ballard, *Appalachian Journal*'s editor, asked an early round of really good questions. Gillian Berkowitz, from Ohio University Press, did the same. George Ella Lyon insisted the spider story was the beginning of this book.

Jules Corriere, another community playwright, contributed the notes on the changes in Colquitt, Georgia, and she contributed to my thinking on agency in a couple of lovely afternoons with good wine and strawberries. Sally Betterton contributed to my thinking about agency in a grade-school classroom. Some good wine and strawberries were consumed then, too. Good wine and strawberries do seem to be useful in the service of agency.

Kathy Sova, my editor at TCG, has done great service for clarity and has encouraged many, many necessary gestures in honor of *The Chicago Manual of Style*. Discursive writing is not what I've been doing for thirty-plus years; if one of my characters says something in a less than grammatical way, who is to argue with me? I've been an editor's nightmare, and the book is much improved for her services. I owe her some good wine and strawberries.

And so we come to a man who is picky about this and that: Al Bentz. His reading is as omnivorous as my own, he is as devoted a student of the new science as I am, and between houses (he's a site supervisor for the local Habitat for Humanity affiliate, and he's picky about that job, too) he's turned an excellent critical eye to what I'm trying to do with this book. Fact-checker is the usual title for the job he has done, but that job with this book has been bigger than the usual fact-checker job. (How many times have you had to argue about what the Heisenberg Uncertainty Principle *really* means?) This is the second of my books he has done such service for (the first was *Teller Tales: Histories* from Ohio University Press), and they are both richer for his participation. I am in his debt for this one.

Many of the community projects for which I've written plays have been produced with Community Performance, Inc. (com-pref.com), first in Colquitt, Georgia, and then with the Mennon-ites in Newport News, Virginia, and many other places. Comm-unity Performance, Inc. has Dr. Richard Geer as director and Jules Corriere (again) as associate director, Iega Jeff (movement) and designers Joe Varga (scene) and Brackley Frayer (lights). Projects in the theater often involve a period of standing and pointing at things very early in a production—this scene goes over there, the emperor can come in over here, etc., etc. (Standing and pointing happens a lot in the construction business, too.) The standing and pointing time in the theater is exceptionally rich for the ideas generated between the disciplines. For me, it is the greatest fun of theatrical collaboration. Nobody has been more fun for the standing and pointing than these folks.

Director Gerard (Jerry) Stropnicky is a founding member of Bloomsburg Theatre Ensemble, and beyond Bloomsburg he has directed for community performance, first with Swamp Gravy, and then with projects which have included my work as play-wright. He's the one who says the community work is "not busi-ness as usual in the black box." Amen.

Thanks to the various communities and the people in those communities who put me in the path of learning, especially to EM and JD and the Mennonite community of Newport News, Virginia.

And to Spider: I do hope this is what you had in mind. If not, please let me know gently, no need to bite me ever again.

Mistakes are all my own.